Leveraging Digital Tools to Assess Student Learning

Leveraging Digital Tools to Assess Student Learning provides a practical approach to using technology to collect, interpret, and curate assessment data in K-12 in-person, online, hybrid, and dual learning environments. Digital media, emerging learning technologies, and handheld devices play larger roles than ever in students' 21st-century educational experiences. Digital tools, meanwhile, can also transform assessment practices for teachers, allowing more efficient means of identifying gaps and modifying instruction to maximize student learning. Situating assessment practices in today's networked, flexible, and virtual classrooms, this book reframes polling and quizzing, social media and memes, and multimedia platforms as digital learning tools for engaging, interactive, and meaningful formative, summative, open-ended, peer and self-paced assessments. The final chapter discusses technology's role in organizing, evaluating, and disseminating assessment data to students, their families, and administrators.

Stephanie Smith Budhai is Associate Clinical Professor in the Teaching, Learning, and Curriculum department in the School of Education at Drexel University, USA, and is certified as a K-12 teacher in Technology Education, Special Education, Information Technology, and Elementary Education.

Student Assessment for Educators

Edited by James H. McMillan,
Virginia Commonwealth University, USA

Using Feedback to Improve Learning
Maria Araceli Ruiz-Primo and Susan M. Brookhart

Using Self-Assessment to Improve Student Learning
Lois Ruth Harris and Gavin T. L. Brown

Using Peer Assessment to Inspire Reflection and Learning
Keith J. Topping

Using Formative Assessment to Support Student Learning Objectives
M. Christina Schneider and Robert L. Johnson

Managing Classroom Assessment to Enhance Student Learning
Nicole Barnes and Helenrose Fives

Using Differentiated Classroom Assessment to Enhance Student Learning
Tonya R. Moon, Catherine M. Brighton, and Carol A. Tomlinson

Leveraging Digital Tools to Assess Student Learning
Stephanie Smith Budhai

For more information about this series, please visit: www.routledge.com/Student-Assessment-for-Educators/book-series/SAFE

Leveraging Digital Tools to Assess Student Learning

Stephanie Smith Budhai

Routledge
Taylor & Francis Group

NEW YORK AND LONDON

Cover image: © Shutterstock

First published 2022
by Routledge
605 Third Avenue, New York, NY 10158

and by Routledge
4 Park Square, Milton Park, Abingdon, Oxon, OX14 4RN

Routledge is an imprint of the Taylor & Francis Group, an informa business

© 2022 Taylor & Francis

The right of Stephanie Smith Budhai to be identified as author of this work has been asserted by her in accordance with sections 77 and 78 of the Copyright, Designs and Patents Act 1988.

All rights reserved. No part of this book may be reprinted or reproduced or utilised in any form or by any electronic, mechanical, or other means, now known or hereafter invented, including photocopying and recording, or in any information storage or retrieval system, without permission in writing from the publishers.

Trademark notice: Product or corporate names may be trademarks or registered trademarks, and are used only for identification and explanation without intent to infringe.

Library of Congress Cataloging-in-Publication Data
Names: Budhai, Stephanie Smith, author.
Title: Leveraging digital tools to assess student
learning / Stephanie Smith Budhai.
Identifiers: LCCN 2021026189 (print) |
LCCN 2021026190 (ebook) | ISBN 9780367354633 (Hardback) |
ISBN 9780367363727 (Paperback) | ISBN 9780429345517 (eBook)
Subjects: LCSH: Grading and marking (Students)–Data processing. |
Educational tests and measurements–Computer programs. |
Academic achievement–Evaluation. | Students–Rating of.
Classification: LCC LB3051 .B7934 2022 (print) |
LCC LB3051 (ebook) | DDC 371.27/2–dc23
LC record available at https://lccn.loc.gov/2021026189
LC ebook record available at https://lccn.loc.gov/2021026190

ISBN: 978-0-367-35463-3 (hbk)
ISBN: 978-0-367-36372-7 (pbk)
ISBN: 978-0-429-34551-7 (ebk)

DOI: 10.4324/9780429345517

Typeset in Sabon
by Newgen Publishing UK

Access the Support Material: www.routledge.com/9780367363727

Contents

List of Figures		vi
List of Tables		vii
1	21st-Century Assessment Practices: A Paradigm Shift	1
2	Questioning, Online Polling, and Virtual Quizzing	25
3	Assessing Learning through Social Media, Memes, and Emojis	48
4	Multimedia Platforms for Open-ended, Peer, and Self-Assessment	72
5	Online Tools to Curate, Evaluate, and Disseminate Assessment Data	99
Index		119

Figures

2.1	Slido Present Video with Submitted Questions	29
2.2	Bloom's Taxonomy	37
5.1	Kahoot!	111
5.2	Yacapa Assessment Application Elements	112

Tables

1.1	From the Field TechAssess Example	7
1.2	From the Field TechAssess Example	8
1.3	4Cs Assessment Type & Sample Tech Tool Matrix	10
1.4	Overview of Diagnostic Assessments	11
1.5	Features of Digital Tools That Can Be Used For Supporting Learner Needs During Assessments	14
1.6	Tips for Getting Started With Using Digital Tools for Assessment	18
1.7	Related Resources and Digital Tools	19
2.1	Categorization of Types of Questions	26
2.2	From the Field TechAssess Example	33
2.3	TechAssess Ideas for the Inclusive Classroom	35
2.4	Question-type Matrix	38
2.5	Now What? How to Get Started	42
2.6	Related Resources and Digital Tools	44
3.1	Definitions of Terms Related to Social Technologies	50
3.2	From the Field TechAssess Example	55

viii List of Tables

3.3	Examples of Using Twitter to Check Students' Understanding	57
3.4	Examples of Using Pinterest to Illustrate Student Learning	59
3.5	Examples of Using TikTok for Students to Apply Their Learning	60
3.6	Using Emojis as Response Choices in Exit Tickets	64
3.7	Using Emojis to Identify Objects	65
3.8	TechAssess Ideas for the Inclusive Classroom	66
3.9	Now What? How to Get Started	67
3.10	Related Resources and Digital Tools	68
4.1	Overview of Open-ended, Peer, and Self-assessment	74
4.2	Performance and Project-based Assessments Through Makerspaces	79
4.3	TechAssess Ideas for the Inclusive Classroom	81
4.4	Ideas and Digital Tools for Peer-assessment Starters Across Grade Bands	83
4.5	From the Field TechAssess Example	85
4.6	Self-assessment QR Code Activities	87
4.7	Tips for Getting Started with Open-ended, Peer, and Self-assessment	92
4.8	Related Resources and Digital Tools	93
5.1	Using Digital Tools to Differentiate Instruction	101
5.2	Curation Tools to Store and Organize Assessment Data	104
5.3	From the Field TechAssess Example	105
5.4	Sample Layout of a Rubric	108
5.5	Rubric Criteria Examples for Open-ended Assessments	109
5.6	Using Digital Tools to Provide Feedback	110
5.7	UDL's Multiple Means of Action and Expression with the Use of Digital Tools	115
5.8	Related Resources and Digital Tools	116

1

21st-Century Assessment Practices

A Paradigm Shift

Assessment in the 21st Century

Assessment and Evaluation are words that K-12 teachers are quite familiar with. Most everything and anything that teachers do with their students must be documented, written up, and data driven. While documenting student learning is important for many reasons, the pressure to always assess can be taxing on teachers. For students, it can take the excitement of learning away, make them anxious, and negatively impact the overall learning environment. Fortunately, assessment in the 21st century does not have to be stagnant, boring, and overwhelming for students and their teachers. Advances in learning technologies present a ubiquitous opportunity to embrace and transform assessment practices. Learning objectives are still what drives instruction, but digital tools can serve as a catalyst in helping students demonstrate their knowledge.

DOI: 10.4324/9780429345517-1

2 21st-Century Assessment Practices

According to the Glossary of Education Reform (2015), assessment is described as "the wide variety of methods or tools that educators use to evaluate, measure, and document the academic readiness, learning progress, skill acquisition, or educational needs of students" (para. 1). Assessment in the 21st century has many of the tenets that were started towards the end of the 20th century. In the 1990s, the principles of Universal Design for Learning were presented by Anne Meyer and David Rose (CAST, 2018). These principles coupled evidenced-based educational practices with brain sciences to develop a comprehensive framework that educators could use to remove barriers that may be in place to restrict students from learning. Assessment practices in the 21st century use similar guidelines in developing different ways, for individual learners, to demonstrate their knowledge.

Assessment of learning can have dual purposes. Where once educators were mostly concerned with whether students have mastered one academic concept in math or science, for example, we now are looking at other soft skill areas that students may need in future careers that may not even exist at this time. The 4Cs of Critical Thinking, Communication, Collaboration, and Creativity is one area of skills that students will need to be fluent in across multiple working environments (Budhai & Taddei, 2015). Students must be able to think deeply about course content, engage in inquiry, and make authentic meaning of concepts. As students gain new knowledge, they must be able to express their learning through written and oral communication. Teaming and peer connections are critical in the 21st century and collaboration between teachers and teachers, students and students, and teachers and students are at the crux of all academic spaces. In any learning environment, students need space to be creative, flexible, and open. Innovation and invention encouraged by teachers can bring forth the demonstration of learning in new and creative ways. In fact, students are expected not only to work creatively with each other, but use creative thinking and processes to explore and invent (National Education Association, 2014).

The ways in which students learn are changing and how we assess them must make similar adaptations and modifications. Paper and pencil as the sole mechanism for carrying out assessments have gradually been replaced by leveraging digital tools to align assessment practices with the innovation and creative spirit of 21st-century teaching and learning. Through this book, I will share ways in which digital technology tools can assist you in gathering assessments, while providing students with diverse opportunities to demonstrate what they have learned.

Before getting into some of the technology tools used for assessment in greater detail, this chapter sets the stage by discussing assessment standards alignment, exploring the different types of assessments, identifying the potential of digital tools to transform assessment practices and considering how technology can level the playing field for linguistically and neurodiverse students. The focus is on showing you why greater use of technology in assessment is needed to more effectively enhance student learning and motivation.

Preparing Students for Academic Growth

All things considered, assessment is simply the tracking of academic growth, or at least it should be thought of this way. As we teach students, we are essentially preparing students for expanding their knowledge and understanding of content and concepts. Teachers need to provide students with a nurturing and supportive academic space, where the environment is built on the goal of academic growth and development for students and not grades. We need to celebrate progress and not perfect scores, while preparing students for success and use formative assessments to make instructional changes. If students feel prepared to take assessments, they will be confident and likely make more progress than if they are nervous, unprepared, and worried about their grades. Progress is the goal, not points, not scores, not grades. Technology and digital tools can be leveraged to help students grow and develop academically. Students can

4 21st-Century Assessment Practices

enjoy preparing for learning and assessments can be an engaging and exciting experience for students.

Assessment Standards Alignment

There is a symbiotic relationship between the learning that takes place in an academic setting and the ways in which teachers gather the extent to said learning. Kulasegaram and Rangachari (2018) capture the essence of this:

> Learning and assessment are inextricably linked. Objectives, delivery, and assessments are the cornerstones of any educational endeavor. Objectives define what needs to be learned; delivery, the ways and means set in place to meet those needs; and assessments, a measure of whether they have been met. Both students and teachers recognize that assessment drives learning, but what that learning is or ought to be depends on the context, decided by the interactions between teachers and students in a framework set to meet societal needs.
>
> (p. 5)

Assessment is not something that is done in isolation. There is a connection between learning that occurs with instruction, which allows for assessment to happen before, during, and after instruction. This of course means collecting a large amount of data, which takes time; something that many educators do not have enough of. Technology tools certainly help in this area, but before going into those specifics, there is an important role of curriculum and instruction in the assessment process.

The Role of Curriculum and Instruction

We know the connection between learning and assessment; and learning happens as a result of instruction based on the curriculum. Many assessments are intentionally aligned with federal and/or state standards, which in the USA is currently guided by the Every Student Succeeds Act (ESSA). The US Department of Education (2015) states that the ESSA guidelines require individual states to develop academic standards specific to their state for particular content and subject-matter areas. There is much flexibility to how states decide to meet the standards; however, it must be aligned with the federal guidelines. As states develop curriculum standards within the overall structure, they must also align assessment activities. Assessments cannot be created in isolation of curriculum and instruction. There needs to be intentional and purposeful planning for assessment that is woven and knitted into the fabric of the standards and lessons. This does not mean that assessments need to be monolithic and stagnant. In fact, curriculum and instruction guidelines can serve as a catalyst in developing new and creative ways for students to show you what they learned, and what they know.

Building Students' Cognitive Presence

Much of assessment practices are geared toward determining if, and to what extent in range, scope, and scale, cognitive activities have been mastered. As mentioned previously, what needs to be mastered is often guided by set standards embedded within the curriculum, that is carried out through instruction. As students move through learning activities, teachers must ensure that students are thinking deeply about concepts and connecting them to other learning experiences. Garrison et al. (2001) created the Community of Inquiry Model, which includes cognitive presence. Through assessment practices, students can be cognitively present while reflecting on their learning in concert with engaging in discourse. Honing in on developing students' cognitive presence throughout instruction has the potential to carry through in assessments that are standards aligned and instruction driven.

Technology's Influence on Assessment Practices

While assessment practices in the 21st century are distinct from those in the past, it is important to recognize that the core purposes of assessment have not changed. Instead, the ways in which teachers go about gathering the assessment data of their students' learning is done in new, and exciting, ways. With the technological advances that have been made in society, it is

6 21st-Century Assessment Practices

possible to leverage some of the digital tools that may have capabilities that can influence today's assessment practices.

Students Do Not Know They Are Being Assessed

One of the most promising influences that technology has had on assessment practices is the gamified-nature of some of the apps and websites. This allows for assessing students without them knowing that they are being assessed. Technology's influence on assessment can turn traditional assessment practices into a game, which really enhances the overall experience and allows for students to demonstrate their knowledge with fidelity and confidence, in a relaxing learning environment, because oftentimes they do not realize that an assessment is taking place. Teachers can then use the data that they have informally collected, to make instructional decisions to move forward with the lesson.

Some students may experience test anxiety (Steinmay et al., 2016), and just the simple fact of knowing that they are being assessed could negatively influence their overall results on the assessment. With technology tools that are game-like, the questions are asked in very exciting ways. A tool, such as Kahoot!, has vibrant music in the background. Use of these assessment tools on mobile applications seems far enough removed from paper and pencil that it does not seem like a test, and students can freely answer. Jeopardy Labs offers online templates for teachers to create assessment exercises that model the popular game show *Jeopardy*.

Promotes the 4Cs and Entrepreneurial Thinking Skills

The 21st-century assessment practices promote the 4Cs and provide students with opportunities to develop their entrepreneurial thinking skills, which is critical for future career readiness (Obschonka et al., 2017). Starting with *critical-thinking*, which requires reasoning, making decisions, and problem solving (Budhai & Taddei, 2015), assessments can be developed in this same way. Mind-mapping assessments allow students to demonstrate their understanding of concepts and ideas as they relate to each other, organize course content systematically, and demonstrate high-level thinking skills. Performance tasks and skill-based and branching scenarios (Sorin et al., 2012) require students to use inquiry skills and problem solve. Simulations (Lateef, 2010) can be designed where students navigate through virtual environments that are based on the real-world settings, and show teachers that they would be able to do so effectively in real life. Table 1.1 provides a From the Field TechAssess example of using the digital tools Smart Learning Suite, Epic! and Prodigy Game to assess students' critical-thinking skills.

Table 1.1 From the Field TechAssess Example

Below is an example of how a current teacher in the field has used digital tools for assessment purposes.

Skill Being Assessed: Critical-thinking

Digital Tools Used: Smart Learning Suite, Epic!, and Prodigy Game

Why I Use the Digital Tool to Assess Student Learning: The learning tools allowed me as a teacher to see immediate responses and to track where my students are academically. Students are way more engaged because they know that I can see if they are participating or not on the digital tool. For example, for the Smart Learning Suite, students have their names attached and then they interact with the presentation. It is basically Google Slides on steroids and way more engaging.

Other Ideas: I also post monthly affirmations behind me for the students to say that align to the school's value of the month. For example: September was Respect/Diversity so the affirmation was "You Always Matter" to know that diversity is beautiful and that everyone matters, no matter what their diversity is. October is Trust/ Honesty so the affirmation is "Be Your True Self" so that students are honest to themselves. Once you're able to be honest with yourself, honesty towards others will come more natural.

Teacher: J.T. Kaltreider, 4th Grade, Philadelphia, Pennsylvania

---

8 21st-Century Assessment Practices

Communication skills are promoted in assessments that require students to show teachers that they are able to express course learning and content understanding both orally and through written methods. Voice-recorded presentations can be prepared by students to present their learning to their teachers, parents, and families. Instead of just doing the presentation once in class, the recorded presentation can be practiced and listened to by the student before submitting to the teacher. The link to the video can be shared to more than just those who were in class during the day of a live presentation. Podcasting is another oral communication assessment activity that students can use to demonstrate their understanding of particular topics. Podcasting combines both oral and written communication, as scripts and talking points are often prepared prior to the recording of the podcasts. Finally, written communication skills can be assessed through online blogging. Table 1.2 provides a From the Field TechAssess example of using the digital tool iCivic on Clever to assess students' communication skills.

Table 1.2 From the Field TechAssess Example

Below is an example of how a current teacher in the field has used digital tools for assessment purposes.

Overview: To assess student learning, I use online tools that include a variety of video, visuals, and presentation materials.

Skill Being Assessed: Communication

Digital Tools Used: iCivics on Clever

Why I Use Digital Tools to Assess Student Learning: Students would have to write notes on their paper. This tool is more effective and interactive.

Other Thoughts: We must use technology effectively to engage learners today and tomorrow.

Teacher: Stephen Thorne, 8th Social Studies, Temple Hills, Maryland

---

Collaboration skills include being an active listener, having the ability to negotiate and peacefully resolve differences of opinions, and working with teams. Putting students on debate

21st-Century Assessment Practices 9

teams and using a rubric to look at specific skills can be done through a technology tool such as Kialo. Critical-thinking skills are also used in these collaborative efforts, and teachers can judge how much students know collectively about the course content through their debate responses. Each student would need to actively listen to the opposing debate teams to ensure they have enough information to craft a rebuttal. The assessment of project-based learning can be created in virtual teams where students will have to work collaboratively to successfully complete the assessment and demonstrate their knowledge to their teachers. Project Pals has a collaborative platform that can be used to create and assess virtual project-based learning teams. Listening skills are critical to working in teams. Websites such as Listenwise can be used for students to develop their listening skills and teachers can assess students' listening skills through the website as well.

The last of the 4Cs, *creativity*, is a 21st-century skill that can be taught (Boyd & Goldenberg, 2013), and assessed through the development of infographics, digital storytelling, and 3D printed models. Through the creation of infographics, students can demonstrate their knowledge and creativity using graphics, fonts, and figures. Video, audio, and links to different URLs can also be embedded into infographics. By assessing students' digital stories, teachers can see if students have the ability to create stories that include specific elements as related to the subject-matter being assessed. The assessment of 3D models created by students can show that students have specific details of the related content accounted for.

There are a myriad of digital tools that can be used to assess students' critical-thinking, collaboration, communication, and creativity skills (4Cs). Table 1.3 provides a matrix that teases out the type of assessment activity and a digital tool that can be used to carry out the assessment to demonstrate fluency of each of the corresponding 4Cs.

10   21st-Century Assessment Practices

Table 1.3 4Cs Assessment Type & Sample Tech Tool Matrix

Type of Assessment Activity (Digital Tool)	Critical thinking	Communication	Collaboration	Creativity
Mindmapping (Mindmeister)	X	X		
Scenario-based Learning (Articulate360)	X			X
Simulations (PraxiLabs)	X			
Voice-recorded Presentations (Knovio)		X		X
Podcasting (AudioBoom)	X	X		X
Online Blogging (Kidblog)	X	X		
Virtual Debate Teams (Kialo)	X	X	X	X
Virtual Team Project-based learning Projects (Project Pals)	X	X	X	X
Listening Skill Development (Listenwise)			X	
Infographics (Piktochart)	X	X		X
Digital Storytelling (Storybird)	X	X		X
Printed 3D Models (Tinkercad)				X

Student Engagement is Embedded in Assessment Practices

When you think about the different technology-infused assessments mentioned above (mind mapping, scenario-based, simulations, voice-recorded presentations, podcasting, online blogging, virtual debate teams, infographics, digital storytelling, and 3D models), they all include elements that naturally engage students in the assessment process. As opposed to having to simply use a pencil to write or circle in responses, when digital tools are used for assessment practices, students are involved in the process, which allows them to share their learning more robustly while enjoying the process.

Understanding the Types of Assessments

There are many ways to assess students' learning. Understanding the different types of assessments is necessary before moving forward with using digital tools to capture assessment data. Different types of assessments have distinct purposes and aims. Some of the types of assessments that are commonly created by teachers and used in K-12 learning include diagnostic, benchmark, formative, and summative. Table 1.4 provides a review of the what, when, why, and how of the types of assessments that K-12 teachers often create or administer, including Diagnostic, Benchmark, Formative, and Summative.

Table 1.4 Overview of Diagnostic Assessments

	Diagnostic
What	A diagnostic assessment can be thought of as a pre-test taken to determine what a student already knows. The types of questions asked in a diagnostic assessment are framed with the purpose of gathering information about what the student already knows, what their skills are, and any areas of concern or gaps that need to be addressed. You can think of a diagnostic assessment as a tool that evaluates students' strengths, weaknesses, knowledge, and skills prior to instruction.

(continued)

12   21st-Century Assessment Practices

Table 1.4 Cont.

When	Since the purpose of diagnostic assessments is to determine what a student's present levels of performance is, they should be conducted at the start of the school year or the start of the marking period.
Why	Diagnostic assessments are used to gain baseline information on students' knowledge, prior to the learning activities and lessons.
How	A diagnostic assessment can be in the form of a formal test, observation, or a combination of the two.

Benchmark

What	A benchmark assessment are those periodic examinations that occur during the school year. You can think of a benchmark assessment as a way of checking in on the student's growth and development.
When	A benchmark assessment is usually scheduled at different periods throughout the year.
Why	A benchmark assessment is conducted to check in and confirm that students are where they need to be, at specific points of time in the school year and, if not, to change instruction in a way to fill in any gaps.
How	A benchmark assessment is carried out either through teacher-made assessments or end-of-unit assessments provided by academic curriculum publishers and test makers.

Formative

What	Formative assessments are those that are integrated checkpoints throughout the learning day.
When	Formative assessments are typically carried out in the middle of the lesson but can also happen at the beginning of the lesson and at the end of the day as exit tickets.
Why	The purpose of formative assessments is to ensure that students are keeping up with the lesson and are learning the content. You would not want to move on to the next concept if students have not understood the first concept.
How	Quick polls, questions, and learning activities embedded into the daily instruction are ways that formative assessment data is collected.

21st-Century Assessment Practices **13**

Table 1.4 Cont.

Summative	
What	Summative assessments are those that measure students' learning after a comprehensive amount of content has been taught.
When	Summative assessments occur at the end of a lesson or unit.
Why	To determine how much learning occurred throughout the lesson or unit, summative assessments are carried out.
How	Summative assessments are usually unit or end of lesson tests that are either teacher made or aligned from the curriculum materials teachers are using.

The Role of Technology in Leveling the Playing Field for Assessing Diverse Learners

Technology can be extremely useful for all students; however, for linguistically and diverse learners, it can be life changing. Universal Design for Learning can be easily adapted into technology-infused classrooms. Digital choice boards for assessments are a great way to provide students with options to complete an assessment that would work best for them. Remember, for any assessments, teachers are trying to measure some skills or learning concept, but the way that information is gathered can be done in a different way. Setting up a digital choice board can be done easily by creating a simple table using Google Docs. Within the table would be choices for a student to complete a specific assessment. The names of the assessments would be hyperlinked to take the student directly to the assessment of their choosing. There are specific features within different technology tools that could assist diverse learners while completing assessments. Table 1.5 describes a few of them.

14   21st-Century Assessment Practices

Table 1.5 Features of Digital Tools That Can Be Used For Supporting Learner Needs During Assessments

---

TechAssess Ideas for the Inclusive Classroom

- **Translation Tools:** For learners who are linguistically diverse, using translation tools within the assessment tool to translate key words is a supported feature within many digital tools. Even if the tool does not have a translation feature, learners can use **Google Translate** for assistance during assessments.

- **Text Highlighting:** Some students have difficulties with focusing and seeing too many words at a time as it can be distracting. The use of highlighting text while students are reading assessment questions and passages can help them focus on the question at hand and not get overwhelmed with other words on the screen.

- **Text to Speech:** For learners who struggle with reading and decoding, text to speech functions can be quite useful to ensure that students have access to assessment questions.

- **Automatic Saving:** Most technology tools used for assessment have auto saving built in. This means that even if students are given additional time to complete the assessment, they do not have to be concerned with the page timing out and their work getting lost.

- **Narrative Explanations:** Tools that have the ability for teachers to include explanations to go along with directions and questions on the assessments can help learners who may struggle with test taking and reading. These narrative explanations can be recorded and played as an audio or video file directly on the digital assessment.

- **Visuals:** Having visuals to go along with typed text is helpful for learners who are more visual. Also, sometimes words can be difficult to decipher but having a corresponding image can help learners make sense of the meanings of the words. Digital assessment tools allow for visuals to be included in addition to text.

Transforming Assessment Practices with Digital Tools

The process of completing an assessment requires multiple layers and understanding of related content. Traditional assessments must be transferred and changed to more comprehensive structures that require deeper learning skills from students (Conley & Darling-Hammond, 2013). Technology has the ability to transform assessments and the overall experience for students. Moreover, with the use of technology, assessments can be integrated directly into the lesson at hand, used to quickly discover gaps in learning, provide teachers the opportunity to make real-time modifications, allow students to guide and track their own learning, facilitate universal design for learning opportunities, and make for a seamless data collection experience.

Integrate Directly into Lessons

The use of technology tools in assessments provides the capability to integrate formative assessment directly into the lesson. For example, presentation slides of a lesson could include poll questions to start the lesson off, and see what students already know. A digital KWL chart (what students know, what students want to know, and what students learned about a particular lesson), can be provided for each student where they type in or use a stylus to complete the digital chart. As the lesson goes on, students can be asked to complete drag and drop or matching questions using a technology platform. Links to URLs can be embedded into the presentation slides or QR codes if students have mobile devices and want to access additional content to support the completion of the assessment.

Quickly Discover Gaps

One of the major purposes of assessing student learning is to confirm if students have mastered course content and, if not, to determine which specific areas of understanding students need to further strengthen. If teachers are not aware of how much the students have learned, their teaching can be in vain. Teachers do not want to move forward with the lesson if the student has not learned the prerequisite knowledge. At the same time, teachers do not want to belabor a topic if students have mastered it. Assessments provide that mechanism to determine if and when students are ready to move along in the lesson. One of the major

16   **21st-Century Assessment Practices**

benefits of using digital tools for assessments practices is the ability to receive instantaneous feedback regarding the student's learning. Teachers can quickly discover gaps that the students have and address them immediately.

Real-Time Instructional Modifications

Once teachers have used formative assessment practices that are directly embedded into the lesson to quickly discover gaps, they can address them immediately by making real-time instructional modifications. Teachers can modify their lesson in real time based on how students score on formative assessments. Making these real-time modifications are beneficial in keeping students on track and not falling behind. Teachers can also pinpoint the specific area(s) that the student may need more support and instruction in to fully understand the concepts. Real-time modifications are similar to why many schools moved from the Discrepancy Model when testing students for special education services to the Response to Intervention (RTI) Model. Instead of waiting for students to fail, teachers can gather data through technology-infused assessments to make real-time modifications during instruction to support student learning.

Student-Guided Tracking of Learning

A soft skill that students are taught in schools is to be self-sufficient and independent. Technology has different student-friendly analytics features that allow students to take ownership in their learning and track how they are doing. Using technology tools for assessment is transformational in that it promotes self-efficacy in students. There are many ways that assessments done using technology can help students. Some programs provide feedback and tips that can help students locate the correct answer. Others will not let students go to the next question until they either attempt to answer the question or answer the question correctly. Having the ability to track one's learning helps students build their autonomy and gives them confidence.

Facilitates Universal Design for Learning Opportunities

Each learner is unique and the way in which they process information and come to learn course content is different from their classmates. Universal Design for Learning (CAST, 2018) provides a comprehensive framework for providing all students access to the curriculum. This is done through the stages of multiple means of representation, multiple means of engagement, and multiple means of action and expression. Simply put, teachers must use a variety of modalities to present content to students, engage students in the lesson, and for the purpose of assessment provide students with diverse options to demonstrate their learning. Digital tools connect with multiple means of action and expression. For example, using a teacher-made Nearpod module in one assessment, students can be asked multiple choice questions, polls, fill in the blanks, or have a blank sketch pad to notate. Students may be great at drag and drop questions but struggle with multiple-choice questions. Having the opportunity to attempt different types of questions within the same assessment will give students the chance to excel at correctly responding to questions that are aligned with their learning style instead of being forced to respond only to the types of questions that they might not always do well with. Also, within the digital assessment, teachers can make easier adjustments of assessments for different learners and include text to speech, color changes, and customize the questions.

Now that an overview of different assessment types and digital tools that can be leveraged to assess student learning has been provided, I encourage you to use the tips provided in Table 1.6 to get started with leveraging digital tools to assess student learning in your own classes.

18 21st-Century Assessment Practices

Table 1.6 Tips for Getting Started With Using Digital Tools for Assessment

Now What? How to Get Started

Now that you have read about 21st-century assessment practices and using digital tools to assess student learning, the next step to get started is to review what you have been doing and prepare yourself for carrying out technology-infused assessments in responsible, practical, and legal ways.

Review current assessments: you are already assessing your students through formative, summative and other ways. Review your current assessments and determine which one might be best to try to administer using a digital tool. The key is to start off with one assessment, and build from there.

Choose a digital tool: Once you have determined which assessment to focus on, think about the ways that you are already using digital tools in the classroom to engage students during the lesson. Pull from the online resources and tools that were mentioned throughout this chapter, or even those that are included in Table 1.7. You will need to have both the assessment in mind and the digital tool in order to move forward with creating and administering an assessment through the use of a digital tool.

Comply with the law: Ensure that you are aware of related laws and acceptable use policies for your school when using digital tools for teaching and learning. Review your school's acceptable use policy and touch base with your school administrator if you are unclear about any aspect of the policies regarding technology use for teaching and learning. Confirm that you have all the appropriate permissions from parents too.

Legal and Ethical Considerations

As we move forward in leveraging digital tools to enhance and carry out assessment practices, it is important to consider legal and ethical guidelines. Two laws specifically that can have an impact on the use of online digital tools are the Child Internet Protection Act, which is known as CIPA and the Children's Online Privacy Protection Rule of 1998, which is known as COPPA. Enacted by Congress in the year 2000, CIPA created requirements for schools and libraries to protect children from consuming obscene content found online (Federal Communications Commission, 2020).

In order to qualify for e-rate funding, schools must have an internet safety policy in place that monitors the online activities of minors and provide education to minors in regard to appropriate behaviors in an online environment. COPPA, on the other hand, requires online websites and programs to disclose when they are collecting and tracking information and data of minors. Permission must be given by parents and, in many cases, schools can provide the permission on behalf of parents.

While the digital assessment tools that you use may not intentionally expose your students to harmful content, some websites may have pop-up ads or links that may take students to suspicious websites. To teach students how to safely navigate online, digital citizenship education should be part of the curriculum and consistently discussed in class. Digital citizenship is touched on again in this book, however, a resource to more content regarding it is provided at the end of this chapter. Teachers should also review websites and digital tools prior to requiring students to use them, and ensure that students understand not to navigate to outside websites or click on unauthorized links. Additionally, websites and tools should be well vetted and ensure that proper permissions from parents have been approved.

Related Resources and Digital Tools

Table 1.7 provides a list of the resources that were mentioned in this chapter, including a brief description and the URL. Use these related resources to expand the context and your understanding of many of the items that have been discussed in Chapter 1.

Table 1.7 Related Resources and Digital Tools

Resource	Description	URL
Articulate360	Scenario-based Learning digital program.	https://articulate.com
AudioBoom	Online Podcasting tool with broadcasting functionalities.	https://audioboom.com

(*continued*)

20 21st-Century Assessment Practices

Table 1.7 Cont.

Resource	Description	URL
Child's Internet Protection Act (CIPA)	The Federal Communications Commission provides the full details of the Child's Internet Protection Act (CIPA).	www.fcc.gov/consumers/guides/childrens-internet-protection-act
Children's Online Privacy Protection Rule (COPPA)	The Federal Trades Commission provides the full details of the Children's Online Privacy Protection Rule (COPPA).	www.ftc.gov/enforcement/rules/rulemaking-regulatory-reform-proceedings/childrens-online-privacy-protection-rule
Digital Citizenship	This website offers a variety of lesson plans for K-12 learners regarding digital citizenship, ethical and appropriate online behaviors, and internet safety.	www.commonsense.org/education/digital-citizenship
Edublogs	Online blogging program for students and teachers.	https://edublogs.org/
Epic!	Digital book and video system that can track students' progress as they engage with the content.	www.getepic.com/
Google Docs	Online multimedia word processing application.	www.google.com/docs/about/
Google Translate	Free tool to translate words in over 100 languages	https://translate.google.com
iCivics	Interactive website focused on civic education	www.prodigygame.com/main-en/

21st-Century Assessment Practices   **21**

Table 1.7 Cont.

Resource	Description	URL
Infographics	Visual content maker with easy to use templates.	https://piktochart.com/
Jeopardy Labs	Online application with templates to create assessments that mirror the Jeopardy game show.	https://jeopardylabs.com
Kahoot!	Learning games, quizzing and polling online application.	https://kahoot.com
Kialo	Online debate and argument mapping site that encourages critical-thinking.	www.kialo-edu.com
Kidblog	Kid-friendly site to publish student writing	https://kidblog.org/
Knovio	Voice-recorded presentation software.	https://knovio.com
Listenwise	Online digital tool focused on improving students' listening skills.	https://listenwise.com
Mindmeister	Online mind mapping tool.	www.mindmeister.com
Nearpod	Multimedia platform for interactive formative assessment within lessons.	https://nearpod.com
Online Exit Tickets	The United Federation of Teachers offers ideas for digital exit tickets.	www.uft.org/news/teaching/linking-learning/using-online-exit-slips

(continued)

22   21st-Century Assessment Practices

Table 1.7 Cont.

Resource	Description	URL
Partnership for 21st Century Learning	This website provides the framework for 21st Century Learning.	http://static.battelleforkids.org/documents/p21/P21_Framework_Brief.pdf
Piktochart	Infographic, presentation, and attractive report maker	https://piktochart.com
PraxiLabs	Virtual and interactive 3D, hands-on simulation tool.	https://praxilabs.com
Prodigy	Online gamified math questions with tools to motivate students.	www.prodigygame.com/main-en/
ProjectPals	Interactive team-based website for project-based learning activities.	www.projectpals.com
Smart Learning Suite	Web-based software to teach and assess student learning.	https://suite.smarttech-prod.com/
Storybird	Virtual creative storytelling tool for young writers.	https://storybird.com
Tinkercad	3D app for design, electronics, and coding.	www.tinkercad.com
Universal Design for Learning (UDL)	Provides the full Universal Design for Learning guidelines with exemplars.	http://udlguidelines.cast.org/

Summary

Assessment is a core part of the educative experience. And while assessment may not be something that students and teachers look forward to, it does not mean that it cannot be an exciting and rewarding experience. By focusing on a students' growth and development, preparing them to demonstrate their knowledge in different ways, and tracking their progress using ubiquitous digital tools, assessment in the 21st century and beyond can take new meaning. Throughout this book, you will learn about the many ways of assessing student learning, while leveraging a myriad of digital tools. In Chapter 2, assessment through online polling and quizzing is focused on. Chapter 3 introduces the idea of social media, memes, and emojis as a way of assessment. In Chapter 4, multimedia platforms for open-ended, peer, and self-assessment are highlighted. In the final chapter, Chapter 5, ideas for curating, evaluating, and disseminating assessment data is discussed. Each chapter also includes:

- **From the Field TechAssess Examples:** In this section, K-12 teachers currently in the field share some of the ways in which they have used digital tools to assess their students' learning.
- **TechAssess Ideas for the Inclusive Classroom:** In this section, ideas are provided for you to differentiate assessments to support the needs of linguistically and neuro diverse learners.
- **Now What? How to Get Started:** This section includes tips and next steps for using some of the ideas and strategies presented in the respective chapters, in your own classrooms.
- **Related Resources and Digital Tools:** This section provides resources related to each chapter's content that will allow you to take a deeper dive into the content and explore different digital tools that can be used to assess student learning.

I hope that as you read through each chapter in this book, you discover new and innovative ways to leverage digital tools to assess student learning.

References

Boyd, D., & Goldenberg, J. (2013). *Inside the box. A proven system of creativity for breakthrough results*. Simon & Schuster.

Budhai, S., & Taddei, L. (2015). *Teaching the 4cs with technology: How do I use 21st century tools to teach 21st century skills?* ASCD Arias.

CAST (2018). *Universal design for learning guidelines version 2.2.* Wakefield, MA: Author.

Conley, D.T., & Darling-Hammond, L. (2013). *Creating systems of assessment for deeper learning*. Stanford, CA: Stanford Center for Opportunity Policy in Education.

Federal Communications Commission (2020). Child Internet Protection Act. www.fcc.gov/file/15349/download.

Federal Trades Commission (2020). Children's Online Privacy Protection Rule. www.ftc.gov/enforcement/rules/rulemaking-regulatory-reform-proceedings/childrens-online-privacy-protection-rule.

Garrison, D.R., Anderson, T., & Archer, W. (2001). Critical thinking, cognitive presence and computer conferencing in distance education. *American Journal of Distance Education*, 15(1), 7–23.

Glossary of Education Reform (2015). Assessment. www.edglossary.org/assessment/.

Kulasegaram, K., & Rangachari, P.K. (2018). Beyond "formative": Assessments to enrich student learning. *Advances in Physiology Education*, 42, 5–14.

Lateef, F. (2010). Simulation-based learning: Just like the real thing. *Journal of Emergencies, Trauma, and Shock*, 3(4), 348–352.

National Education Association (2014). Preparing 21st century students for a global society: An educator's guide to the "Four Cs". http://dl.icdst.org/pdfs/files3/0d3e72e9b873e0ef2ed780bf53a347b4.pdf.

Obschonka, M., Hakkaraninen, K., Lonka, K., & Salmela-Aro, K. (2017). Entrepreneurship as a twenty-first century skill: Entrepreneurial alertness and intention in the transition to adulthood. *Small Business Economics*, 48(3), 487–501.

Sorin, R., Errington, E., Ireland, L., Nickson, A., & Caltabiano, M. (2012). Embedding graduate attributes through scenario-based learning. *Journal of the NUS Teaching Academy*, 2(4), 192–205.

Steinmayr, R., Crede, J., McElvany, N., & Wirthwein, L. (2016). Subjective well-being, test anxiety, academic achievement: Testing for reciprocal effects. *Frontiers in Psychology*, 6, 1–13.

US Department of Education (2015). Every Student Succeeds Act. www.ed.gov/essa?src=rn.

2

Questioning, Online Polling, and Virtual Quizzing

Why Question?

During academic instruction, we spend time introducing and reinforcing content and concepts to students, but how do we know if students are taking in and absorbing what we are sharing with them? Simply put, teachers use questioning. Questioning can create excitement for students and encourage critical-thinking and creativity. According to Mehta and Fine (2019) classroom contexts can sometimes be described as "a game of 'cover-remember-test-forget-repeat' that occupies students' and teachers' time but produces little sustained understanding" (p. 199), which is less than ideal. While teachers seemingly ask more questions of students, part of being critical thinkers requires students to also question and inquire (Andarab & Mutlu, 2019). Stagnation and tradition can stifle the beauty of learning; how we go about assessing students can become equally stale if we ask questions in the same traditional ways.

DOI: 10.4324/9780429345517-2

26 Questioning, Online Polling

In the 21st century, with the use of technology as a mechanism tool, questioning provides opportunities to go beyond the traditional cycle of teaching and learning, and provide new and exciting ways to determine what students know and have learned as a result of instruction. There are different ways to ask questions, and Mehan (1979) provides a seminal perspective on discourse in the classroom. Categorized in four areas of choice, product, process, and metaprocess, questioning in the classroom can be looked at through this framework. Table 2.1 describes each of the four areas.

Table 2.1 Categorization of Types of Questions

Choice	"Ask students to agree or disagree with what the teacher said in the previous turn, and so merely depends on students' recognition of correction information or guessing" (Nathan & Kim, 2009, p. 96)
Product	"Invites students to provide factual knowledge, such as a name or place, which they must generate from long-term memory" (Nathan & Kim, 2009, p. 96)
Process	"Asks students to provide opinions or interpretations" (Nathan & Kim, 2009, p. 96)
Metaprocess	"Asks students to connect their responses with the intentions of a teacher's elicitation by providing, for example, the justification supporting a student's reasoning" (Nathan & Kim, 2009, p. 96)

Questioning is at the crux of formative assessment and a major part of the instructional day. With the use of digital technology tools, we can question students in different ways, and have students take part in asking questions. The more students inquire about learning concepts, the better positioned they are to experience deeper learning. Deep learning occurs when teachers ask students questions, regardless of the complexity, that they are already thinking about and have some thoughts on (Mehta & Fine, 2019). Next, we will explore online polling and multimedia quizzing as new approaches that can enhance effective questioning.

Online Polling

Polling, in the general sense, is used to get the opinions of others. There may be a topic or idea that you want to administer a poll on, to gauge how the public views it. On the other hand, online polling, which is what we will focus on, in the classroom environment, goes beyond trying to gain the collective opinions of others. Within classrooms, online polling can be used to question students and learn what and how they are thinking about content. Online polling is similar to Clickers technology and has been found to benefit students by helping them self-monitor their own understanding of course content (Egelandsdal & Krumsvik, 2017). There are many different digital online polling tools that can be used on computers, tablets, and mobile phone devices, and a wide variety of types of polling questions are available.

Purpose

The purpose of online polling in the classroom is related to assessment practices and its ability to collect real-time formative assessment data. Online polling with real-time responses can advance assessment and engagement practices in the classroom (Sarvarym & Gifford, 2017). Teachers can set up online polls as part of a diagnostic activity, with the goal of determining what students already know about a topic. Online polling can afford teachers the ability to gain quick, but meaningful, data points about how students are doing. Through online polling, students are engaged in their learning (Sarvarym & Gifford, 2017), and have the opportunity to contribute to the class environment.

Types

Online polling can be administered in a few ways. One popular way of polling is to ask a question to students with options for them to select from. This is similar to how a multiple-choice test question may be asked. Students will choose one of the answer choices and then typically a chart or graph will appear on the next screen to show the percentage of students who choose

28 Questioning, Online Polling

each of the response options. Online polling can also be asked through open-ended questions. This would require students to type their responses out using a word or even sentence format if the question requires a longer response. Some online polling tools offer a blank canvas for a response, with doodling features. This would be helpful for either young children to draw their response or older students if the response requires a depiction of something or an image. Quick true or false polls can also be asked within online polling as well as fill in the blank. With fill in the blank polls, there could be answer choices or just a blank line embedded in the question, where the teacher would be able to learn what students are thinking through the words they embed.

Uses

A digital tool such as an online poll can serve as a formative assessment measure and provide teachers with information needed to give students additional support (Smith & Mader, 2015). Online polling can also engage learners during the lesson and be used to check students' understanding of content before, during, and after the lesson. If using online polling before the lesson, polling questions can give teachers a sense of students' prior knowledge. Having this type of baseline data is important and can assist in tracking students' growth. It would be difficult to know how much students learned from the lesson without having an idea of where they started from. During the lesson, online polling can be used as periodic check-ins to make sure students are keeping up with the lesson and grasping the new ideas being presented. Another use of online polling during the lesson is to get students' feedback on how they are thinking about the content, with the ability to share their ideas and thoughts. In a traditional classroom where students would raise their hands to share their thoughts, it would be difficult to get every students' feedback. However, with online polling, every student can have a voice and teachers can go back and review the data of how each student responded to the poll questions. As illustrated in Figure 2.1, students can also use online polling to ask questions. After the lesson, online polling questions can capture students' overall learning and growth. Since you conducted pre-lesson polling, the data can be measured to account for growth.

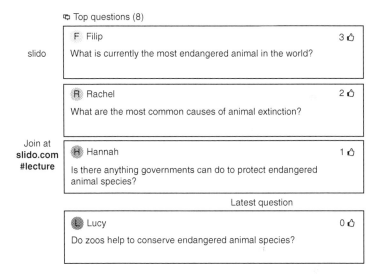

Figure 2.1 Slido Present Video with Submitted Questions
Source: Slido.

Advantages

Not only does online polling keep students engaged in the learning process, it can also serve as a practice of testing skills and prepare students for summative tests (McGivern & Coxon, 2015). Students can become acquainted with item formats, and gain familiarity in responding to the many different types of polling questions that they may see on an actual quiz. Online polling can also be used to test out future quiz questions. How questions are written is just as important as the question itself, and sometimes students may answer a question incorrectly because of how it is worded. Online polling provides an

30 Questioning, Online Polling

authentic opportunity for teachers to gain awareness on how students are understanding the question asked by examining the corresponding responses. If students who teachers know should respond a certain way to a poll question do not, then the teacher may need to look at rewording the question. This is great for revisions of planned test questions. Different types of polling questions can be administered, which adds variety to the online polling experience. Students may grow tired of responding to the same type of polling question each time. Having the ability to change how the question is asked and the types of questions will increase student engagement and serve as a catalyst to getting more substantive responses.

Considerations When Creating Polls

While there are many advantages to using online polls to collect formative assessment data, such as the positive impact on students' metacognitive skills (Molin et al., 2020), there are considerations when creating polls that should be taken into account. These challenges can be ameliorated and prepared for, however, understanding some of the roadblocks that you may be faced with when using any digital tool for assessment purposes will be helpful to successful implementation.

Anonymity of responses: Teachers can decide if they want to anonymize online polling responses, which can be an advantage to students who want to share their learning but may be afraid of doing so with their name attached to the response. Many online polling tools allow for the poll response to be hidden to the class but shared with the teacher only. Teachers can also give students a number or polling pseudonym name that they will use when responding. Students would need to keep this information private if they do not want their classmates to be able to identify them. While offering students the opportunity to share what they know anonymously can be encouraging for those who may be shy or too nervous to participate in front of other classmates, if the responses are anonymous, you do not know which specific student may need further support with gaining content and application knowledge. One way around this is to assign students with a pseudonym or number that is associated with their real name. In this case, only the teacher and student would know that number 5, for example, is connected to a student named Emmet Johnson. Students would need to be told to keep their number or pseudonym private from other students, and only their parents and teacher should be aware.

Limited devices: It is great for students to be able to participate in online polling before, during, and after a lesson. Depending on teacher and student access to devices such as computers, tablets, and smartphones, there may not be enough devices for each student to participate at the same time. If limited devices are a reality for your learning community, think about pairing students or putting them in small groups. Have several rounds of polling questions where each student in the pair or team has an opportunity to respond. Another option is to save online polling for small group instruction, where there would likely be enough devices for everyone in the learning group.

Onboarding: If you are using a new tool, it can take time to set up the first time. Once you use the tool a few times, students will get used to it and connecting to the tool to participate in the poll should be more seamless. When choosing online polling tools, try to start with those that do not require hardware to be downloaded to a device. Use online polling tools that can be easily accessed through a short alphanumeric code, link, or QR code. When using technology for any aspect of teaching and learning, focus on one tool at a time, versus introducing students to too many tools at once. You do not want students to become frustrated with the technology, and negatively impact their assessment and overall learning experience.

Time limits: One of the nice features of online polling is that polls can be integrated within the lesson, between content slides, in any course. Since teachers typically have a set amount of time to teach different subjects each day, there is a limit on the amount of time students would have to respond to polling questions. Some students may need more time than others to process the question, think about the answer, and then record their response. Depending on how much time you give students to respond, learners who need more time to process may not

32 Questioning, Online Polling

be able to participate in the online poll. To avoid leaving out learners, use online polling for questions that are short and would not require lengthy open-ended responses. Multiple-choice question online polls should be limited to three choices. You can also use pictures for answer choices with some tools, such as Kahoot!, instead of words.

Virtual Quizzing

In its simplest form, quizzing is the act of asking questions. The questions being asked require an answer; however, there are many types of answers. A virtual quiz has the same goal and purpose as a traditional quiz; however, it is completed electronically and has features that are not possible with pencil and paper. Sometimes the words "quiz" and "test" are used synonymously, but they are not exactly the same. Quizzes typically are much shorter than tests, covering a smaller amount of content.

Purpose

The purpose of quizzing in the classroom is to provide students with the opportunity to share what they know about course content, while also helping teachers determine potential gaps that need to be addressed before moving forward with introducing new content. Quizzes can serve as preparation for longer tests, and research has shown that taking quizzes can help students reduce potential anxiety that is associated with test taking (Khanna, 2015). With the vast features that virtual quizzing provides, such as real-time feedback and at-the-moment correct answers, students and teachers can make good use of the practice of routine and regular virtual quizzing.

Types

There is no one standard form for virtual quizzing; the types of virtual quiz options are truly endless. One common type of virtual quiz is set up like a traditional quiz, where there are approximately 7–10 questions asked. These questions may be in the form of multiple choice or true and false, where students would simply click their answer choice using the device they are working on. Virtual quizzes may also be set up using drag and drop features or fill in the blank type answers. If drag and drop is not available, students can simply type or draw the word in the blank area within the quiz question.

Advantages

Virtual quizzing provides several advantages when compared to traditional paper and pencil quizzes. With the expansion of one to one and BYOD programs in schools, students might already have a technology device for the lesson. This makes it easy to have students scan a QR code (Burns, 2016) or go to a saved website to complete a quiz during the lesson. These types of accessible and embedded virtual quizzes can serve as a meaningful checkpoint for both students and teachers. Also, if the lesson or unit is extended and will take multiple weeks, virtual quizzing can be used as an immediate check point to help break up content, and reinforce previously learned concepts as the lesson goes on. It is also more simple to modify quizzes based on a student's IEP or for students who are English-language learners when they are available virtually. Table 2.2 provides a From the Field TechAssess example of an emotional support teacher who uses online Boom Cards as a digital questioning formative assessment tool.

Table 2.2 From the Field TechAssess Example

Overview: After concluding week 1 of "Zones of Regulation" instruction, students were asked to complete an assessment to identify which zone the person was in when he/she was expressing a specific feeling or emotion.

Skill Being Assessed: Self-Regulation

Digital Tools Used: Boom Cards

(*continued*)

34 Questioning, Online Polling

Table 2.2 Cont.

Why I Use Digital Tools to Assess Student Learning: I choose to utilize Boom Cards as a digital assessment tool because it helps to keep students engaged during the assessment. Students seem to also enjoy the graphics, visuals, and audio that is provided during the assessments. Graphics, visuals, and audio also help to increase student focus during assessments. At the end of the assessment a teacher report is generated with details of student progress which helps to provide the teacher insight on what skills were mastered and what skills need to be retaught.

Other Thoughts: If a Boom Cards assessment was not utilized for this assessment, I would have utilized a multiple-choice questionnaire to assess students' understanding of each specific zone. The assessment would have included visual emotion cards that would allow students to first identify the emotion, then identify the specific zone/category that the emotion would fit in.

Teacher: Genice Matos, 2–4th Grade Emotional Support, Limerick, Pennsylvania

---

The functionality of online polling and virtual quizzing allows students different ways to respond to the questions. Depending on the specific digital tool used, students can click or highlight answers, use a drag and drop feature, type out their answers using a keyboard, or even use a drawing tool to respond to quiz questions. For teachers, the automatic grading of most polling and quizzing tools allows for more time spent on providing valuable feedback to students. Many virtual polling and quizzing tools also have reports that summarize individual or group progress over time. Using online polling and quizzing also saves on printing out polls and quizzes and physically filing scored polls and quizzes. All student work can be housed electronically and easily shared with parents. Finally, in addition to all of the advantages of using online polling and virtual quizzing for all students in the classroom, there are a few adjustments that can be made to ensure that students with disabilities, English-language learners, and learners who need extra support can benefit from digital tools used to gather assessment data. Table 2.3 describes those.

Questioning, Online Polling **35**

Table 2.3 TechAssess Ideas for the Inclusive Classroom

Online Polling

- **Drawing Tool**. Instead of requiring learners to type their responses, encourage them to use the drawing tool feature of an online polling application. This way, learners who are non-verbal, have limited English language proficiency, or learners who are not able to put words together, can still participate in the formative assessment activity.

- **Limit Questions**. Try not to have an online poll question that asks more than one question. Only administer one poll question at a time during the lesson, especially at the beginning of the school year.

- **Home Practice**. Before executing a live online poll in the class, have students try the polling tool at home with a family member. This will help students become familiar and comfortable with the tool, and is another way to connect families to the learning that is taking place at school.

- **Polling Partners**. Use a buddy system and pair learners who may struggle academically with a peer who has a stronger grasp of the content. The buddy can assist with navigating the online polling tool, reading the question, and in general being there as a support for their polling partner.

- **Account for Response Time**. Students need time to process information, as well as reading the polling question for understanding. When determining how much time you will give students to respond to the online poll, make sure you have accounted for students who may need additional time to respond.

Virtual Quizzing

- **Use Word Banks**. To assist learners with a limited vocabulary, word banks could be available and on the screen during virtual quizzes. Students would still need to choose the correct answer choice, but their options would be limited to what is in the word bank, which can help them focus.

- **Drag and Drop**. Instead of having students type in the answers, set up the quiz response choices using drag and drop options. Students will not need to worry about erasing if they change their response, and dragging and dropping the answer choice may create a more interesting experience for students during the virtual quiz as it may simulate gaming.

(continued)

36 Questioning, Online Polling

Table 2.3 Cont.

- **Modify Quiz Questions.** Digital quiz tools will allow for teachers to easily modify a master quiz for specific learners. You can adjust the difficulty level of certain questions, and either increase or decrease the number of quiz questions asked for the majority of the class. This would be helpful to learners who are struggling as well as learners who are advanced and need to be challenged.

- **Scaffold Questions.** Sometimes when there is a long line of questions on the screen, students can get overwhelmed; only show one question at a time so students can focus.

- **On Screen Digital Aids.** For mathematics-related quizzes where calculation is required, an on screen calculator could be used. For English language arts quizzes, a digital dictionary and thesaurus could be useful to students during their virtual quiz.

Creating Quality Questions

We have discussed the ways in which online polling and virtual quizzing can be used to gather informal and formative assessment data from students before, during, and after the lesson. Given that there are so many different types of questions, it is important to consider the ways in which we formulate questions, the primary purpose of, and the advantages and disadvantages of each question type. Creating quality quiz questions will enable you to effectively assess what is intended to be assessed. Questions should be aligned with specific learning outcomes that we are trying to determine if students have met. There are also certain question types that should be avoided, if possible, as they often result in unclear and confusing questions for students. We do not want students to spend more time decoding the way in which the question is asked, than they do focusing on the content of the question.

Bloom's Taxonomy

Bloom's Taxonomy of Educational Objectives (Anderson et al., 2001) is a framework that provides a hierarchical structure of the levels of learning outcomes. Figure 2.2 provides an illustration of how learning objectives go from the lower levels of remembering and understanding, to the mid-levels of application and analyzing, to the upper levels of evaluation and creation. For the most part, the online polling and virtual quizzing we discussed in this chapter would fall into the lower–mid levels of Bloom's Taxonomy of Educational Objectives. In Chapter 4, we will look more intently at open-ended and performance-based assessments that are geared towards assessing students learning at the upper levels of Bloom's Taxonomy of Educational Objectives.

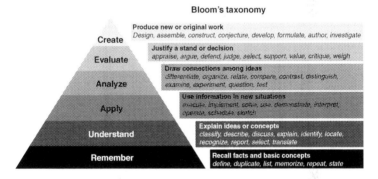

Figure 2.2 Bloom's Taxonomy

Source: Vanderbilt University Center for Teaching (under a Creative Commons Attribution license).

Question Type Matrix

There are a variety of question types available, and the most used and offered through digital tools seem to be fill in the blank, multiple-choice, open-ended, and true/false type questions. Table 2.4 below is a question type matrix that provides a description of each type of question, an example of how that question could be written, and both the advantages and potential drawbacks of using each question type. As you create questions for assessments in your classroom, revisit this matrix to select the appropriate question type to use and when.

38 Questioning, Online Polling

Table 2.4 Question-type Matrix

Question Type	Description	Example	Advantages	Drawbacks
Fill in the blank	Questions that require the answer choice to be filled in to one or more lines within a sentence or paragraph. Some fill in the blank questions may have a word bank.	There are ___ number of states in the United States of America.	Can be used to assess if students can recall facts and vocabulary words.	Students may need more context clues or the support of a word bank.
Multiple choice	Questions that provide multiple possible answer choices where the test taker has to choose the best answer choice.	How many months are in one year? a. 1 b. 12 c. 9 d. 11	Provides students with hints of what the correct answer might be, if they are familiar with the content.	Students can successfully guess the correct answer through process of elimination, without actually fully understanding the question being asked.

Open-ended	Questions that do not have any answer choice options and require longer written responses. Typically, the test taker will need to add evidence and details to support their response.	In 3–5 sentences, explain what causes a rainbow.	Allows the instructor to assess how much the student knows about the topic. Questions can get at the higher level of Bloom's Taxonomy.	Takes a great deal of time for students to take the assessments and for instructors to grade the assessment.
True/False	Questions where there are only two responses options: true or false.	True or False: In order of operations, addition problems should be completed before multiplication problems.	Can be used for quick formative assessments during the lesson.	There is a 50% chance of answering every question correctly, so the instructor will not know if the student is guessing.

40 Questioning, Online Polling

What to Avoid in Quiz Questions

Some multiple choice questions can be flawed due to ineffective writing (Przymuszała et al., 2020). To maintain reliability in responses, certain types of questions should be avoided, including double-barreled questions, none of the above questions, all of the above questions, and negative questions.

Double-barreled: A double-barreled question asks about two different issues, but only allows for one answer choice. For example, a true or false double-barreled question would include, "The main character in the story was the fastest runner *and* most popular student in the school". The issue here is that if the main character was in fact the fastest runner in school but not the most popular, or the reverse of this, the question could not be accurately answered. It is best to ask questions that only address questions about one item.

None of the above: Particularly in multiple-choice questions, asking students questions that have none of the above as an answer choice will not tell you as the teacher if the student has met the learning outcome. Students can also become overwhelmed with going through all of the answer choices and may second guess themselves, thinking that none of the answer choices are correct since there is a none of the above answer choice.

All of the above: Similar to none of the above questions, all of the above questions should not be used unless absolutely necessary to assess whether the student has met the learning objective. If you do decide to use all of the above questions, be sure that the answer choices will not "trick" students.

Negative phased questions: When questions are written using negative phasing, students can sometimes get confused. Try to avoid using negative phased questions such as "which of the following is not true about the life cycle of reptiles?". If negative phased questions must be used to meet the learning objectives, write it as "The life cycle of reptiles includes all of the following stages except".

Online Polling and Virtual Quizzing Considerations Across Different Grade Bands

Using online polling and virtual quizzing can be done across K-12 grade level students, but there are some considerations to keep in mind that are specific to younger versus older students.

Elementary level: For elementary students who are still expanding their vocabulary and gaining reading fluency, it may be helpful to use pictures instead of words or in addition to words in the online polling questions. Some online polling applications, such as Mentimeter, allows for video to be played to support a question, and this may be helpful for younger students in understanding the question that is being asked. It may also be helpful to have younger students practice with polling using low tech options, before utilizing polling for assessment. During a live synchronous session, you could ask students to respond to simple agree or disagree questions and have them hold up sticks or hands to share their response. This will get them used to participating in a poll. For virtual quizzing for younger students, try to limit the number of questions asked and write concise questions. Utilize digital applications such as Quizizz that allow for audio and/or video directions to be embedded into the question.

Middle and secondary level: For middle and secondary students, it is important to set ground rules for participating in online polls. Older students may want to be silly and post inappropriate responses to gain laughs from their peers. Have a discussion with older students first about the importance of giving authentic responses to polling, since you as the teacher need to be able to get an accurate glimpse of their learning in order to adjust instruction. It may be helpful to use an online polling tool with profanity filters and moderation features such as Poll Everywhere. Middle and secondary students can also

42 Questioning, Online Polling

take ownership in the process of creating poll questions. Not only would this provide students with a chance to spend more time with the content, but they will also feel more connected to the lesson and can develop other 21st-century skills such as critical thinking and communication.

Now that you have read about the many ways in which online polling and virtual quizzing can be used in K-12 classrooms, the next step to get started is to decide on what learning outcomes you would like to assess students on. Even though this book has a focus on providing many digital tools that can be used to capture assessment data, learning outcomes are still at the forefront. Once you have decided on the knowledge, awareness, and skills that you will assess students on using an online poll or virtual quiz, tool selection is the next step. Use the information provided in Table 2.5 as you plan.

Table 2.5 Now What? How to Get Started

Compatibility: Depending on what type of digital tools are available to you and your students, it is important to confirm which type of devices are compatible with the online polling or virtual quizzing digital tool you select. The tool can have all of the features you are looking for and at the right price. However, if it only works on tablets and your students only have access to Chromebooks, then you would not be able to use that tool. In addition to determining whether the device is compatible with the devices your students have access to, determine if the program is web-based or requires software to be downloaded.

Cost: Prices of digital tools have wide ranges. Some offer free and paid versions, while others are either only free or require a school or site license. Know what your school's technology budget is, and if you would be able to purchase the tool if a fee or license is required. If there is a limited budget, start with tools that offer a free version. Many educational technology companies offer steep discounts for educators.

Features: Each online polling and virtual quizzing tool will have unique features. Determine what features you need to gather the assessment data. Are you looking for an online polling tool that allows for open-ended responses? Do you want a virtual quiz tool

Questioning, Online Polling **43**

Table 2.5 Cont.

that uses drag and drop and word bank features? Determine the type of online polls and virtual quizzes that you want to create and then cross-reference to see if the digital tool you are hoping to use has those features.

Analytics reporting: Having the data of how your students responded to polls and quizzes is key. Review the analytics reporting features for the polling and quizzing tools you are interested in. Check if they provide reports for the class as a whole and/or individual student reports. You should also check how detailed the reports are, if they include charts and graphs, and how they can be accessed.

In Table 2.6 are several online polling and virtual quizzing digital tools that you can use to get started. See if any of those meet your needs and start questioning your students to discover what they know!

Related Resources and Digital Tools

Table 2.6 provides a selection of online polling and virtual quizzing digital tools that you can explore and use in your classrooms to collect assessment data before, during, and after the lesson.

Summary

Online polling and virtual quizzing provide engaging and interactive ways to assess what students know prior to the lesson, what they are learning during the lesson, and how their overall learning has changed by the end of the lesson. Through the use of digital tools to poll and quiz students, gaps and areas to spend more time on can be made in real time during the lesson. It is important to craft quality questions that clearly align to learning outcomes. I encourage you to explore the resources and digital tools mentioned above and throughout the chapter, as well as utilize some of the ideas provided in the TechAssess Ideas for the Inclusive Classroom section (Table 2.3) to ensure that all of your students can benefit from and enjoy online polling and virtual quizzing as you gather information on their learning. In the next

44   Questioning, Online Polling

Table 2.6 Related Resources and Digital Tools

Tool URL	Free Version Available	Polling	Quizzing	Three Key Features
Answer Garden https://answergarden.ch/	YES	YES	NO	(1) Focused on asking open-ended questions that lend themselves to short responses (2) No login required (3) Unlimited number of responses
Boom Cards https://wow.boomlearning.com	YES	NO	YES	(1) Self-grading feature (2) Gamified (3) Includes sound
Crowd Signal https://crowdsignal.com/	YES	YES	NO	(1) Fonts and colors can be customized (2) Filters available to analyze data (3) Ability to export data into Google Sheets spreadsheets
Kahoot! https://kahoot.com/	YES	YES	NO	(1) Can reuse and edit existing Kahoot! Created by other teachers (2) Real-time formative assessment of learning (3) Visual reports can be produced showing students' progress
Proprofs www.proprofs.com	YES	YES	YES	(1) Sets up automatic periodic reminder to test takers (2) Ability to upload documents and notes directly into the quiz (3) Can create customized certificates

Quizizz https://quizizz.com/	YES	YES	YES	(1) Uses gamification to engage learners in answering quiz questions (2) Embeds polling questions directly into the lesson (3) Individual quizzes can be assigned to students to complete at home
Quizlet https://quizlet.com/	YES	NO	YES	(1) Uses flash cards to ask questions (2) Can be used as an in-class study game (3) Has a database of questions related to science, arts and humanities, math, and social science
Mentimeter www.mentimeter.com	YES	YES	YES	(1) Images and gifs can be added to poll and quiz questions with free stock image and GIF libraries (2) Can translate questions into Spanish, French, German, and Portuguese (3) Uses profanity filters in multiple languages
Poll Everywhere www.polleverywhere.com/	YES	YES	NO	(1) Six question types (2) Option for polling from web or PowerPoint (3) Feedback appears in real time on each slide
Slido www.sli.do	YES	YES	YES	(1) Seamless integration with Google Slides (2) Has a timer feature to answer questions (3) Includes a leader board for class challenges

(*continued*)

46 Questioning, Online Polling

Table 2.6 Cont.

Tool URL	Free Version Available	Polling	Quizzing	Three Key Features
Socrative www.socrative.com/plans/	YES	YES	YES	(1) Gamified quiz questions (2) Up to 20 poll and quiz activities can be activated at once (3) Students log in using student ID
Vevox www.vevox.com/	YES	YES	YES	(1) Live quiz option with leader board (2) Anonymity polling responses (3) Integration with PowerPoint slides
Yacapaca https://yacapaca.com/	TRAIL	NO	YES	(1) Database has over 22,000 teacher-written assessments (2) Used artificial intelligence to auto mark responses (3) Aligns assessment questions with learning objectives

chapter, we move our focus to using social media, memes, and emojis to assess student learning.

References

Andarab, M.S., & Mutlu, A.K. (2019). Student questioning in literature circles: An investigation of forms of questioning among ELT students. *Journal of Language and Linguistic Studies*, 15(1), 326–338.

Anderson, L.W., Krathwohl, D.R., & Bloom, B.S. (2001). *A taxonomy for learning, teaching, and assessing: A revision of Bloom's Taxonomy of educational objectives* (Complete ed.). Longman.

Burns, M. (2016). *Deeper learning with QR codes and augmented reality: A scannable solution for your classroom*. Corwin.

Egelandsdal, K., & Krumsvik, R.J. (2017). Clickers and formative feedback at university lectures. *Education and Information Technologies*, 22(1), 55–74.

Khanna, M. (2015). Ungraded pop quizzes: Test-enhanced learning without all of the anxiety. *Teaching of Psychology*, 42(2), 174–178.

McGivern, P., & Coxon, M. (2015). Student polling software: where cognitive psychology meets educational practice? *Frontiers in psychology*, 6(55), 1–3.

Mehan, H. (1979). *Learning lessons: Social organization in the classroom*. Cambridge, MA: Harvard University Press.

Mehta, J., & Fine, S. (2019). *In search of deeper learning: The quest to remake the American high school*. Harvard University Press.

Molin, F., Haelermans, C., Cabus, S., & Groot, W. (2020). The effect of feedback on metacognition – A randomized experiment using polling technology. *Computers and Education*, 152, 1–21. doi.org/10.1016/j.compedu.2020.103885.

Nathan, M.J. & Kim, S. (2009). Regulation of teacher elicitations in the mathematics classroom. *Cognition and Instruction*, 27(2), 91–120.

Przymuszała, P., Piotrowska, K., Lipski, D., Marciniak, R., & Cerbin-Koczorowska, M. (2020). Guidelines on writing multiple choice questions: A well-received and effective faculty development intervention. *SAGE Open*, 10(3), 1–12.

Sarvarym, M.A., & Gifford, K.M. (2017). The benefits of a real-time web-based response system for enhancing engaged learning in classrooms and public science events. *Journal of Undergraduate Neuroscience Education*, 15(2), 13–16.

Smith, B., & Mader, J. (2015). Formative assessment with online tools. *The Science Teacher*, 82(4), 10.

3

Assessing Learning through Social Media, Memes, and Emojis

The Role of Social Technologies in Assessment Practices

Social technologies in education have brought together educational communities in meaningful ways related to teaching and learning (Davey & Tatnall, 2013). Through social technologies, interactive and vibrant learning opportunities for students have been made possible. While once considered something that may not be the most appropriate technology tool for academic settings, the use of social technologies has increased in K-12 schools. The National Association of Secondary School Principals (2020) has recognized the ubiquitous nature of social technologies used in education and has created guidelines and recommendations for school leaders in ensuring that social technologies are used responsibility in schools with the aim of providing students with opportunities to consume, create, and share their learning.

DOI: 10.4324/9780429345517-3

Given that social technologies are being used for teaching and learning, it is important to look specifically at how social technologies can be used for students to demonstrate their knowledge and show teachers what they have learned as a result of their teaching. Broadly defined, social technologies are interactive, participatory, and collaborative technology tools that provide virtual spaces to consume content and connect with others, regardless of geographic locations. Social technologies can be fun, engaging, exciting, and are widely used across many different age, income, and racial demographics. Social technologies are constantly emerging, so instead of focusing on specific tools, it is important to center the attention of this chapter on how different types of social technologies can be used in education settings to assess learners, as opposed to how specific tools can be used. In this chapter you will find sample social technologies that you can try out.

One advantage of using social technologies is that different social technology digital tools have features and formats that connect with a multitude of intelligences that students may work best with. Garner (2006) named several and among them is interpersonal intelligence. In this respect, students with high interpersonal intelligence have the ability to connect with others and be productive. In a school setting, this would include working on teams, collaborating on projects, and openly listening to the perspectives of peers. Students with strong interpersonal intelligence may thrive in environments that include social technologies. At the same time, students who may not have strong interpersonal intelligence may build those skills if the use of social technologies is connected to learning. In addition to tapping into students' interpersonal intelligences, the use of social technologies relies on audio, video, images, and verbal aspects. This means that students with high auditory-musical, visual-spatial and verbal-linguistic intelligences have the opportunity to flourish in environments that use social technologies. In this chapter, the focus is on how different social technologies, including social media, memes, and emojis, can be used to gather assessment data and provide different engaging and creative ways for students to show you what they know.

50 Assessing Learning

Defining Terms

There are new and emerging terms to describe the various aspects of social technologies. A list of the ones that are relevant to this chapter are described in Table 3.1. As you read through the chapter, feel free to refer to the list for a reminder.

Table 3.1 Definitions of Terms Related to Social Technologies

Term	Definition
Artificial intelligence	"The science and engineering of making intelligent machines, especially intelligent computer programs. It is related to the similar task of using computers to understand human intelligence, but AI does not have to confine itself to methods that are biologically observable" (McCarthy, 2007, p. 2).
App	The shortened form of the word "application", and is a software program designed to be used on mobile devices such as cellular phones and tablets. Some apps also work on computers.
Avatar	A digital character that represents a persona of a person (An et al., 2013).
Bitmoji	Cartoon-like avatar versions of people (Lacoma & Beaton, 2020).
Chatbots	"Computer programs that simulate human conversations through voice commands or text chats and serve as virtual assistants to users" (Luo et al., 2019, p. 937).
Creative commons	A non-profit organization that allows creative material to be shared freely and legally.
Digital citizenship	"Norms of appropriate, responsible behavior with regard to technology use" (Ribble, 2015, p.15).
Direct message (DM)	A message that is sent privately to users on different social media platforms.
Emojis	A character with faces and objects that represents something that is used in online communication (Das et al., 2019).

Assessing Learning 51

Table 3.1 Cont.

Term	Definition
Emoticons	Short for emotion icon, emoticons are a typographic display that is used to convey emotion in online communication.
Filter	Software that changes the original appearance of an image.
Geotag	Online geographic tracking of locations of images and apps based on where the user is located (Cramptona et al., 2013).
Handle	A username on social media platforms that usually has an @ before the name.
Hashtag	"A hashtag – written with a # symbol – is used to index keywords or topics on Twitter. This function was created on Twitter, and allows people to easily follow topics they are interested in" (Twitter, 2021, para. 1).
Meme	"A virally transmitted image embellished with text, usually sharing pointed commentary on cultural symbols, social ideas, or current events. A meme is typically a photo or video, although sometimes it can be a block of text" (Gil, 2020, para. 1).
Meme generator	Technology tool that is used to create memes.
Microblogging	Frequent and short messages posted online.
Notification	Digital alert that a message is waiting to be read.
Social media	Internet-based two-way communication platforms that used videos, images, text, and audio to connect with others.
Tweet	A message that is posted on the Twitter social media site.
Vlog	Video version of a blog.

Digital Citizenship

There are many apprehensions by teachers, administrators, parents, and even some students, about the use of social media within academic learning contexts. These concerns are certainly not unwarranted, as there are security issues that have permeated online environments. Additionally, cyberbullying – acts of cruelty, harassment, and hate, using electronic methods – are also concerning. Because of these potential misuses, it is important to ensure that students are well aware of the responsibility required to communicate, engage, and learn within the World Wide Web and through social media platforms.

Many students and teachers have created virtual lives that are both distinct and similar to the way they live in the real world. Just as there are local, state, and federal laws that guide how people behave, work, and live, the online world has its own set of rules, norms, and expectations. Ribble (2015) shares nine elements of digital citizenship, including digital access, commerce, communication, literacy, etiquette, law, rights and responsibilities, health and wellness, and security. In broader society, being a good citizen means following laws and contributing to society. In concert with this, some of the aspects of being a good digital citizen include:

- **Safe practices:** This includes students having a comprehensive understanding of what it means to be safe in online environments. Students must know that they are not to go to unauthorized websites, engage with adults, not including their teachers, and that they should not give out their private information online.
- **Privacy:** Protecting the privacy of passwords and personal information such as names, social security numbers, and addresses, is part of being a good citizen. Students should know that they are never to share their personal information with anyone, and should create complex passwords that they can remember, but cannot be easily guessed.
- **Appropriate communication:** There are so many different ways to communicate your thoughts and perspectives in

online environments. Students must know who to communicate with online, when to communicate with them, how to communicate with them, and what to communicate. Profanity or harmful words should never be used.

- **Copyright:** Students must understand what copyright is, and how to give credit for work if they decide to cite someone else's work in their assignments.
- **Content consumption:** Students must be critical consumers of content, and know that not everything found on the internet is true. Good digital citizens understand that there are different types of content, and authors, and how to decipher trusted sources.
- **Respectful behaviors:** Good digital citizens are kind to others in the words they type, the images they share, and their verbal communication through audio and video. Students interact, communicate, and use social technologies within an online environment in a responsible manner. The term "netiquette" falls into this domain, and also covers being selective in sharing, responding to "all", and sending large files via email.

Being a good digital citizen has some of the same attributes as being a good person. Preparing students to be good digital citizens can help ensure that they have the knowledge, awareness, and skills needed to safely and effectively contribute to digital communities.

Social Media as a Digital Assessment Tool

Social media is a type of social technology that "encompasses all those forms of digital technology that allow us to communicate information or content with each other using the internet" (Poore, 2015, p. 3). Social media has been used to provide information in and out the classrooms – among other things, disseminating news and world events, posting inclement weather school closings, and even sharing health information (Bliss, 2015). In addition to social media being used to disseminate information to others and engage in discourse, it also has the potential to be

54 Assessing Learning

used as a way to reinforce concepts (Teixeira & Hash, 2017), as well as to gather assessment data. The qualities that identify social media according to Poore (2015) include: collaboration, community building, communication, creativity, customization, distribution, flexibility, interactivity, networking, participation, and sharing. You will notice that three of the 4Cs that were discussed in Chapter 1, are qualities of social media.

There are many advantages to using social media in education. Most social media tools are free, which lessens the burden of educators looking for digital tools but have a limited budget. Social media tools are ubiquitously available and many students and teachers may already be familiar with how to navigate them. If a particular social media tool has not been used by a student or teacher, they are typically user friendly and easy to learn. Since using social media tools requires the 21st-century skills of communication, collaboration, and creativity (Poore, 2015), students can also build those skills while engaging with fun and interactive digital tools, all while being assessed. Students can also select tools that connect with their linguistic, musical, bodily-kinesthetic, and interpersonal intelligences (Gardener, 2006).

While there are many advantages to using social media in education, there are also inherent challenges. Cyberbullying can occur when engaging with other students while on the internet. We hope that students will all behave as good digital citizens and refrain from unkind actions while online. There is also the chance of inappropriate content and popup ads that can appear online. Teachers must ensure that the social media sites that they are using to assess learners are properly vetted and have appropriate privacy features. Many social media tools, such as Twitter and Pinterest, allow for private pages that can only be assessed by the owner and those who are given permissions to view. Finally, some parents and educators may not associate social media with education and may be apprehensive about its use in schools. Explaining to parents and colleagues on how social media will be used for assessment, the 21st-century skills that students will be building on, as well as the privacy protections that are put into place, will help ameliorate some of their concerns. Table 3.2 provides a From the Field TechAssess example that uses video to assess students' social media knowledge. You may want to conduct a similar assessment activity as you prepare students for appropriate use of social media in the classroom.

Table 3.2 From the Field TechAssess Example

Below is an example of how a current teacher in the field has used digital tools for assessment purposes.

Overview: The students had to record a video of themselves talking about the positives and negatives of social media. I was assessing students' knowledge of social media. We have been discussing social media for some weeks and this was their chance to show me what they learned and be able to add their own take on what we were talking about. They were able to use the camera on their Chromebooks because every student was provided a Chromebook at the beginning of the year.

Skill Being Assessed: Social Media Knowledge

Digital Tools Used: Cameras on Chromebooks

Why I Use the Digital Tool to Assess Student Learning: If it was not done with a digital tool they would have to write a journal or speak in front of the class about what they have learned. I chose this partially out of necessity; however, I considered having students create the video with a camera anyway. I feel they would be more open and honest in front of a camera instead of peers. I wanted to get as authentic an answer as possible.

Other Ideas: Use what people already have, many students already have access to a camera.

Teacher: Malik Macon, K-8th Grade Media, Philadelphia, Pennsylvania

---

Checking Students' Understanding through Social Media Tools

In this section, the Twitter, Pinterest, and TikTok social media platforms are described, with different ways that assessment data can be gathered to check students' understanding of concepts and provide students with a means to illustrate and apply their learning. The examples cover a wide range of subject areas and K-12 grade bands.

56 Assessing Learning

Twitter

Twitter is a social media platform that is used to communicate and share short messages through postings known as tweets. While Twitter is primarily used for social networking, educators can incorporate Twitter into their formative assessment efforts to check students' understanding of content, concepts, and processes. There are many ways students can send a tweet. First, they can do so through the traditional typing of words. While the character limit for Tweets was originally set at 140, it has now been expanded to 280. The expanded character limitation will allow students, particularly middle and high schoolers, to respond to a teacher's prompt or question using a longer response, providing more details, where applicable.

Twitter also has a feature to record audio tweets. This option would be helpful for students who are still learning to write language and or who would struggle with the fine motor skills required to type traditional tweets. Videos and pictures can also be uploaded and sent as a tweet in lieu of typing text. All of these possibilities open up many opportunities for students to demonstrate their knowledge, in a fun and engaging way. If parents and/or students do not want to have their tweet responses show up on the class Twitter page or feeds, then they can send you a direct message (DM) with the information. The DM would be private and only the teacher and student would have access to it.

Students would need a technology device to tweet. They can use their cell phones if allowed in school, a tablet, Chromebook, or other laptop. Teachers can respond to the tweets quickly during class, or respond after class when they have more time. Since Twitter limits the number of characters that can be in a tweet, even if there are 25 students in the class, it will only take a few minutes to respond to each students' tweet. Table 3.3 below provides examples of using Twitter to check students' understanding of English-language arts, mathematics, science, and social studies content, across elementary, middle, and high school grade levels.

Table 3.3 Examples of Using Twitter to Check Students' Understanding

Grade Level	*English-Language Arts* After reading a short story, novel, or having a story read to them, students would use the class Twitter page to:	*Mathematics* After working on grade level appropriate operations and algebraic thinking content, students would use the class Twitter page to:	*Science* Focusing on physical sciences content, students will use the class Twitter page to:	*Social Studies* Focusing on civics and government content, students will use the class Twitter page to:
Elementary school level	Name the main character(s) of the story.	Respond to a one- or two-digit addition question that is posted by the teacher on Twitter.	Respond to true/false questions about forces and motion.	Tweet one example of an action that a responsible citizen would take.
Middle school level	Briefly explain the main idea of the book.	Tweet an answer to a multi-step mathematical problem	Share one way that Newton's Third Law can be applied to designing a solution to a problem	Briefly explain the difference between local and state government.
High school level	Describe the author's point of view.	Rewrite (tweet) an algebraic expression.	Post a mathematical representation that illustrates what happens to the total momentum of a system if no net force acts on the system.	Define the word "diplomacy" in their own words.

58 Assessing Learning

Pinterest

Pinterest is a social media platform focused on using pictures as a way to locate information and ideas on a myriad of topics. Images that are found online can be "pinned" to a person's Pinterest board. Generally, a person would have more than one Pinterest board. Pinterest can be used as a curation site, which could house student work in a shareable space for other teachers, peers, and families, but also for assessment purposes. One feature of Pinterest that could be used to protect the privacy of posted student work are secret boards. Secret boards are only accessible and viewable by the person whose work it is, and anyone that they invite to view. Teachers can set up secret boards for students and send links only to other teachers and families. In this way, the students' posted images will not appear in any public search or home feed.

Pinterest also has flexibility in the way that boards are set up and organized. Students will have the ability to drag and drop images, sort alphabetically, and automatically save to the last time they were saved. Additionally, notes can be left on the boards, which would be helpful when using Pinterest for assessment practices. Students can post an image and leave a note for the teachers explaining what the image is and how they are thinking about the image, or teachers can leave feedback to students right on the image. Teachers can help students set up a Pinterest account at the beginning of the school year that they will use throughout the year for various assessments, as described in Table 3.4, to illustrate their learning. The amount of time that students will spend on Pinterest will be determined by the assessment activity. There is a different amount of time that would be required for students to create an annotated photo journal, demonstrate their understanding of processes, or gather artifacts for a portfolio of their collective work. Teachers can provide feedback to the students' Pinterest boards directly on Pinterest by using one of the notes features or can write feedback within the class learning management system. Chapter 5 discusses ways to use digital tools to provide students with feedback on different types of assessments. Teachers can also show each students' Pinterest board during family conferences to discuss assessment data.

Assessing Learning **59**

Table 3.4 Examples of Using Pinterest to Illustrate Student Learning

Annotated photo journal	Students can create a secret (private) Pinterest board with images that reflect their development and understanding of a specific topic throughout the marketing periods. Students will use the notes feature within Pinterest to annotate their images, add information about particular areas that they are struggling with, and tips for remembering large concepts (for example, PEMDAS – Please Excuse My Dear Aunt Sallie – for remembering order of operations in mathematics). Keeping an annotated photo journal is a great way to review concepts and content, and prepare for future assessments.
Demonstrate processes	Pinterest is an innovative way for students to demonstrate their learning and understanding of processes. For example, teachers could create an assessment activity where students would have to locate and pin images to a Pinterest board showing the phases of the moon. In an art class, students could use a Pinterest board to demonstrate their understanding of steps in creating a portrait, from sketching to final product. For high school students taking trades classes, they use a Pinterest board to show the parts of a business plan or computer programming.
Portfolio	Pinterest is a great option to curate student work. Portfolios can be created for the school year, term, or project-based. Teachers will have the ability to look at a wide range of student work, all curated in one place digitally, and assess student growth.
Family conferences	It is important to review and discuss students' assessments and learning with their families. Using Pinterest and inviting families to view students' boards or sharing a screen with families during the family conferences is a great way for families to visualize students' assessments. Teachers can use the notes feature to highlight specific work of the student too.

60 Assessing Learning

TikTok

TikTok is a mobile application that is used to create short-form videos. There is no set template for TikTok videos and the person who is making the video has no boundaries in terms of creativity. Although TikTok is a social media tool, it has been used in different settings to get mass messages to the public, influence thought, and introduce products. In regard to education, TikTok seems to work very well when there is something to be explained, described, demonstrated, or for breaking down steps. Because of this, TikTok provides a unique opportunity for students to apply and demonstrate their learning. Table 3.5 provides a few examples of the types of videos students can make using TikTok in English-language arts, mathematics, science and social studies. Depending on the grade level and how much detail is expected by the teacher, the length of the videos can be modified accordingly. Teachers can use the different ideas in Table 3.5 and assign assessment activities based on the students' created TikTok videos as aligned with a corresponding rubric.

Table 3.5 Examples of Using TikTok for Students to Apply Their Learning

English-Language Arts	*Mathematics*
• Show understanding of the definitions of vocabulary words by creating a video using household objects (e.g. holding a piece of paper to describe the word "light" and point to the "stove" to describe the word "heavy"). • Act out a scene of a seminal play or literary piece (e.g. *Hamlet, A Raisin in the Sun, Julius Caesar, Romeo and Juliet*).	• Visually show geometric angles, shapes, and sizes (e.g. showing a 90-degree angle using arms or legs, pillows, or shoes). • Demonstrate understanding of weight equivalencies (e.g. showing several objects that are equal, such as a one-gallon bottle next to two half-gallon bottles).
Science	*Social Studies*
• Film the process of a plant going through photosynthesis. • Complete a full science lab experiment.	• Detail historical events and time stamps. • Explain the executive branches of the government in a creative way.

Memes as a Digital Assessment Tool

Memes have become a cultural phenomenon that are often seen within social media networks to communicate ideas. A meme is "a virally transmitted image embellished with text, usually sharing pointed commentary on cultural symbols, social ideas, or current events. A meme is typically a photo or video, although sometimes it can be a block of text" (Gil, 2020, para. 1). Most students and educators have seen a meme at some point in their lives, even if they did not know the technical name for them. The use of memes is boundaryless. According to Isaacs (2020), "marketing agencies use memes as tools to try to create viral marketing campaigns. Politicians use three-word slogans, which are memes, to simplify complex messages" (p. 497). Memes are of worldwide use and have impacted society in unique ways.

Because of the broad scope and widespread use of memes, they have the potential to be applied in education. Hinchman and Chandler-Olcott (2018) state in the International Literacy Association's *Journal of Adolescent & Adult Literacy* that memes have "become increasingly common in online discourse, with subject matter ranging from depictions of cats that lighten our days and make us laugh aloud to send-ups of political issues that make us understand these issues in new, more nuanced ways" (p. 249). Memes provide students the opportunity and platform to demonstrate their learning in unique, interesting, and exciting ways on almost any topic.

Memes to Demonstrate Learning

How teachers decide to use memes for assessment purposes will depend on what is being measured and the students' grade level. Teachers may want to locate appropriate memes for students to demonstrate their learning or allow students to create from existing pre-approved memes, from a database such as Impflip Meme Generator. In the following sections, descriptions of memes that can be used to gather assessment data at the elementary, middle, and high school levels are shared.

62 Assessing Learning

You can view the meme examples that are explained in the sections below by accessing the QR code below with your mobile device, or by visiting tinyurl.com/3dj3npms, or downloading a zip folder containing all of the image files at routledge.com/9780367363727. Note: All memes were created using the Impflip Meme Generator (*https://imgflip.com/*).

Elementary School Level

Using a popular "character", elementary level students can be provided with a blank meme where they must appropriately label what the person/character of the meme is feeling based on their non-verbal cues, nouns associated with certain emotions, and opposites. For example, Figure 3.1 could be used to assess whether students know the meanings of the words "happy" and "sad", or if they understand the physical emotion that is displayed when a person is happy or sad. Figure 3.2 could be used to assess whether students understand how people typically react to certain types of events and lived experiences. Figure 3.3 can also assess students' understanding of the words "smile" and "tears" as opposites. See the QR code and URL above to access Figures 3.1, 3.2, and 3.3).

Middle School Level

At the middle school level, students could be challenged to use complex vocabulary where they would be required to attach an appropriate adjective to the meme and write a corresponding sentence. Teachers can provide a word bank, have students only use vocabulary words that they are currently working on, or use the assessment to gather baseline data on how expansive students' vocabulary is. For example, in Figures 3.4, 3.5, and 3.6, the student would use a meme that displayed an accurate definition of one of their vocabulary words. In the first example, Figure 3.4, the vocabulary word is "perplexed". The student then could add a sentence at the bottom of the meme where they use the word "perplexed" in a sentence. Figures 3.5 and 3.6 illustrate the vocabulary words "frightened" and "excitement". See the QR code and URL above to access Figures 3.4, 3.5, and 3.6).

High School Level

For older students, memes can be used to assess students' understanding of historical times, places, and events as well as images that are associated with historical structures. Depending on students' maturity levels and the amount of time that there is for the assessment, teachers can either provide students with memes to choose from or allow students to locate an appropriate meme that depicts a historical time (Figure 3.7), place (Figure 3.8), or event (Figure 3.9). Students can use a meme generator tool (see Table 3.10), to add captions depicting factual elements. The teacher can provide a meme without a caption (Figures 3.7–3.9), but labeled as below, or have students properly label and provide a caption (Figures 3.10–3.12). See the QR code and URL above to access Figures 3.7, 3.8, 3.9, 3.10, 3.11, and 3.12).

Emojis as Assessment Tools in Early Elementary Classrooms

Depending on your younger students' maturity and ability levels, they may not be ready to participate in creating memes

64 Assessing Learning

or use social media to demonstrate their knowledge. The use of emojis may be an appropriate starting point for using the types of social technologies discussed in this chapter for younger learners. The National Association for the Education of Young Children (NAEYC) and the Fred Rogers Center for early learning and children's media created a joint position statement guiding the use of technology for younger learners. The statement asserts that "many strategies of joint engagement and media mentorship are recommended, such as co-viewing of media; asking children questions about a game they are playing; or creating a digital story with a caregiver to document and share an event that happened during the school day" (Paciga et al., 2017, p. 4). Through these recommendations, technology and media use with younger learners for assessment purposes can happen in concert and under the direct mentorship of their teachers.

As shared in the definition of terms (Table 3.1), an emoji is a character with faces and objects. While emojis are primarily used in online communication, they have the potential to be used for informal assessments including as response choices in exit tickets to determine how students feel about their learning after a lesson (Table 3.6) or at the end of the day, as well as to check students' ability to identify different objects (Table 3.7).

Table 3.6 Using Emojis as Response Choices in Exit Tickets

Student Name:

Topic: Adjectives

Directions: Circle the emoji to share how you felt about today's lesson on adjectives.

1) I enjoyed the lesson on adjectives: 😁   😐   😕

2) I know what an adjective is: 😁   😐   😕

Bonus: If you circled the smiley emoji 😁 in question #2, write an example of an adjective

---

Assessing Learning **65**

Table 3.7 Using Emojis to Identify Objects

Directions: Circle the emoji that represents the word listed

Fruit: Strawberry	Modes of Transportation: Helicopter

Sports Ball: Basketball   Animals: Monkey

Social media and networking sites, memes, and emojis are all exciting real-world virtual tools that can also be used in different educational environments. We always want to make sure that we are thinking about ways to include all of our learners in the activities that we create. Our students who may be neurodiverse, need extra support, or who are English-language learners, can also benefit from engaging with social technologies and teachers can use them as a mechanism for students to demonstrate their learning and show teachers what they know. With the use of the constructs of Universal Design for Learning and Differentiated Instruction, we can ensure that all of our students have an opportunity to experience using these social technologies. Table 3.8 shares ways that emoticons can be used for students to demonstrate their learning, as well as the potential for chatbots to serve as virtual instructional supports.

Setting Up Safeguards

Social media, memes, emojis, and other social technologies can be exciting for students, impactful to their learning, and a way to gather assessment data. While most of these social technology digital tools are simple to implement, it is important to assure that proper safeguards for our students are implemented, including protecting their privacy, following the school's acceptable use policy, getting parental consent, and being aware of potential data collection and analytics that applications, websites, and software are tracking.

66 Assessing Learning

Table 3.8 TechAssess Ideas for the Inclusive Classroom

Using emoticons to demonstrate understanding

There may be students who are non-verbal, may experience speech and language challenges, or who may be very reserved when asked to expressively communicate. Short for emotion icon, emoticons are a typographic display that is used to convey emotion in online communication. Emoticons are bright and fun, and can be used in different assessments. For example, you have a social-emotional learning unit and you want students to respond by associating a description of an emotion, with the appropriate visual. In this case, students can have a bank of emoticons to choose from. When you read the description of happy, the student would use the happy emoticon from the word bank to respond. You could also have large versions of emoticons available to students through a tablet that they use throughout the day to point to, or physically printed cards if in the traditional classroom setting. Students can use the emoticons to respond to questions about how their classmates are feeling and to demonstrate that they have an understanding of different emotions.

Working with chatbots for virtual support

As mentioned above in the definition of terms, chatbots are "computer programs that stimulate human conversations through voice commands or text chats and service as virtual assistants to users" (Luo et al., 2019, p. 937). While students may have a teacher assistant and one-to-one academic support available to them during the school day, when not at school completing homework or during a remote learning, a chatbot can be extremely useful in helping students move along with content. The chatbot can respond to questions, offer examples, and provide details that students can use to solve problems. There are dozens of chatbot tools available and there are also programs for teachers who want to create their own. One example of an education app chatbot is Miao. The Miao chatbots can assist students in math and science, by responding to questions. If students still need additional help after the questions are answered, the chatbots provide additional video and online resources.

Of particular concern are the following:

Privacy is extremely important and protecting students' information and data must always be at the forefront. Proper vetting of any social technology tool must happen before using

Assessing Learning 67

it for assessment and all privacy features and filters should be activated.

Parental consent should be received and parents should feel comfortable with the use of the social technologies being used. Consider creating an alternate assessment for students who do not have parental consent. Oftentimes, however, at the beginning of the school year schools will receive parental content from parents for all digital tools that will be used.

Adherence to Law and Policies must always be followed. In Chapter 1 we covered legal considerations, and specifically looked at the Child Internet Protection Act (CIPA) and the Children's Online Privacy Protection Rule (COPPA). Be aware of those laws and also follow your school's acceptable use policy.

Now that you have read about how to use social media tools, memes, and emojis to gather assessment data, the next step to get started is to figure out what exactly you want to assess, and what type of data would be needed. Table 3.9 provides five steps that you can take.

Table 3.9 Now What? How to Get Started

1. **Decide on subject area**: Since social media tools, memes, and emojis can be used to gather assessment data across various academic disciplines, you will first need to decide which subject area to focus on. Once you have the subject area that you want to focus on, you can narrow it down to the topic.

2. **Pinpoint topic**: Once you know which general subject area you would be assessing, decide on the specific topic. For example, you know that you are going to focus on science. Be specific if it is physical, biological, or environmental science, and then provide specificity on what topic within those areas of sciences, the assessment will be based on.

3. **Connect to a learning objective**: One of the major aims of any assessment is to determine whether students have met the learning objectives. When creating an assessments using social media, memes, and emojis, you must have the learning objective in mind that you are assessing learners on.

(continued)

68 Assessing Learning

Table 3.9 Cont.

4. **Choose a social technology category:** Now that you know what the learning objective that you will assess learners on to see if they have mastered, choose which social technology tool you will use. Will you use a social media tool, a meme connected assessment, or something that includes the use of emojis or emoticons?

5. **Locate a specific tool to use:** Once you have determined which category of social technology you will use, locate the specific tool. For example, if you have chosen the social technology category of social media, you need to choose if that will be Twitter, TikTok, Pinterest, or another social media tool that could be leveraged to collect assessment data.

Related Resources and Digital Tools

There were several digital tools mentioned throughout the chapter. Table 3.10 provides a list of social technology tools organized by category. Each digital tool includes a brief description of its use, and corresponding URL. Feel free to use them as you use social, memes, and emojis to assess student learning.

Table 3.10 Related Resources and Digital Tools

Name	Use	URL
Bitmoji/Emoji Creation Tools		
Bitmoji	To make personal emojis that are reflective of self-image	www.bitmoji.com/
Emojicopy	Database of emojis that can be resized	www.emojicopy.com/
iEmoji	Provides a database of emojis with meanings organized by categories	www.iemoji.com/
Smiley.cool	Emoticons with that symbols that can be used in blogs and on social media	https://smiley.cool/emoticons.php

Assessing Learning **69**

Table 3.10 Cont.

Name	Use	URL
Chatbot		
Miao	Artificial intelligence application that used chatbots to assist students with different learning content	www.miaoacademy.org/miao-chatbot
Meme Generators		
Iloveimg	Compress, resize, and crop image capabilities.	www.iloveimg.com
Imgflip	Can create memes, gifs, and charts.	https://imgflip.com/memegenerator
Kapwing	Has video meme maker capabilities.	www.kapwing.com/meme-maker
Lumen5	Users can upload their own pictures to create memes, as opposed to using ones that have been recycled on the internet.	https://lumen5.com/tools/meme-maker
Social Media Sites		
Backchannel Chat	Live chat application designed for classrooms	http://backchannelchat.com/
Pinterest	Online database of visuals that can be connected and shared	www.pinterest.com/
TikTok	A video-sharing social networking application	www.tiktok.com/en/
Twitter	Microblogging tools that allows for short messages to be sent online through text, audio, and video	https://twitter.com/home?lang=en

Summary

Social technologies provide innovative and exciting ways to gather assessment data from students. Through the use of social media sites, memes, emojis, emoticons, and chatbots, students can creatively show their teachers what they know. Because of

70 Assessing Learning

the public and varied use of social technologies, teachers must be aware of protecting students' privacy and information. Additionally, students must be made aware of and trained on digital citizenship, so they are equipped with the knowledge and skills required to responsibly communicate and engage with others online. I hope that you will use the list of tips in the *Now what? How to get started* section (Table 3.9), and try one assessment that utilizes a social media site, a meme, or emoji. In the next chapter, the focus is on open-ended, peer and self assessments through multimedia platforms.

References

An, L.C., Demers, M.R.S., Kirch, M.A., Considine-Dunn, S., Nair, V., Dasgupta, K., Narisetty, N., Resnicow, K., & Ahluwalia, J. (2013). A randomized trial of an avatar-hosted multiple behavior change intervention for young adult smokers. *JNCI Monographs*, 47, 209–215.

Bliss, K. (2015). Social media in the classroom: an experiential teaching strategy to engage and educate. *Pedagogy in Health Promotion*, 1(4), 186–193. https://doi.org/10.1177/2373379915578862.

Cramptona, J.W., Graham, M., Poorthuis, A., Shelton, T., Stephens, M., Wilson, M.W., & Zook, M. (2013). Beyond the geotag: situating 'big data' and leveraging the potential of the geoweb. *Cartography and Geographic Information Science*, 40(2), 130–139.

Das, G., Wiener, H.J.D., & Karelas, I. (2019). To emoji or not to emoji? Examining the influence of emoji on consumer reactions to advertising. *Journal of Business Research*, 96, 147–156.

Davey, B., & Tatnall, A. (2013). Social technologies in education – an actor-network analysis. In: Ley, T., Ruohonen, M., Laanpere, M., & Tatnall A. (eds) *Open and social technologies for networked learning. OST 2012. IFIP advances in information and communication technology*, vol. 395. Berlin, Heidelberg: Springer. https://doi.org/10.1007/978-3-642-37285-8_17.

Gardner, H. (2006). *Multiple intelligences: New horizons in theory and practice*. Basic Books.

Gil, P. (2020). What is a meme? *Lifewire*. www.lifewire.com/what-is-a-meme-2483702.

Hinchman, K., & Chandler-Olcott, K. (2018). Memes. *Journal of Adolescent & Adult Literacy*, 62(3), 249–251. https://doi.org/10.1002/jaal.918.

Isaacs, D. (2020). Memes. *Journal of Pediatrics and Child Health*, 56(4), 497–498. https://doi.org/10.1111/jpc.14755.

Lacoma, T., & Beaton, P. (2020). What is bitmoji? Digital Trends. www.digitaltrends.com/mobile/what-is-bitmoji/.

Luo, T., Tong, S., Fang, Z., & Qu, Z. (2019). Frontiers: Machines vs. humans: The impact of artificial intelligence chatbot disclosure on customer purchases. *Marketing Science*, 38(6), 937–947.

McCarthy, J. (2007). *What is artificial intelligence?* Technical report, Stanford University, http://jmc.stanford.edu/articles/whatisai/whatisai.pdf.

National Association of Secondary School Principals. (2020). *Using mobile and social technologies in school*. www.nassp.org/top-issues-in-education/position-statements/using-mobile-and-social-technologies-in-schools/.

Paciga, K., Donohue, C., & Myers, K.S. (2017). *Highlights from technology and interactive media for young children: A whole child approach connecting the vision of Fred Rogers with research practice*. Latrobe, PA: Fred Rogers Center.

Poore, M. (2015). *Using social media in the classroom: A best practice guide* (2nd edn). Sage.

Ribble, M. (2015). *Digital citizenship in schools: Nine elements all students should know* (3rd edn). Washington, DC: International Society for Technology in Education.

Teixeira, S., & Hash, K.M. (2017). Teaching note—tweeting macro practice: social media in the social work classroom. *Journal of Social Work Education*, 53(4), 751–758.

Twitter (2021). How to use hashtags. https://help.twitter.com/en/using-twitter/how-to-use-hashtags.

4

Multimedia Platforms for Open-ended, Peer, and Self-Assessment

Introduction

As you have seen from the first three chapters of this book, there are a myriad of ways to use digital tools to assess student learning through questioning, polling, quizzing, and social technologies such as memes, social media, and emojis. Often it is important to not only determine what students know, but understand how deeply they have grasped concepts, and the depth of supporting information that can be provided. We want to gather data on how well students can recognize how their peers have met learning objectives, as well as their ability to provide value-added feedback to others. Finally, we want students to be able to engage in self-assessment, where they check their own

DOI: 10.4324/9780429345517-4

Multimedia Platforms 73

understanding of content, reflect on their learning, and use the information to improve their performance on future assessments.

It is well documented that classroom assessments go beyond traditional testing, as "testing is one method of evaluating progress and determining student outcomes and individual student needs" (Overton, 2012, p. 3). Much of the testing that we see in K-12 schools is based on federal and state agencies through standardized assessments or from education publisher curriculum materials. However, as you have already seen in the first three chapters of this book, assessments can be dynamic and more engaging by leveraging digital tools. Many of these more engaging assessments are open-ended and performance-based. Sienkiewicz (2018) describes performance-based assessments as being open-ended assessments that address both academic and 21st-century learning skills, relevant and real-world content, requiring critical thinking, creation, and design. Teachers can contribute to the development of these types of student assessments.

In addition to open-ended assessments, this chapter covers both peer and self-assessment. Because open-ended, peer and self-assessments all have many components, they are especially aided by using multimedia platforms and resources. Multimedia platforms that incorporate a combination of audio, video, text, doodling, and sharing tools can provide students with different options for demonstrating scope and depth to their responses to open-ended assessment questions, can serve as a platform for peer-assessment, as well as a space for reflecting on one's own learning. Table 4.1 provides an overview of open-ended, peer, and self-assessment practices, including the benefits and potential challenges. This will serve as a primer as we continue the discussion on each throughout this chapter.

74 Multimedia Platforms

Table 4.1 Overview of Open-ended, Peer, and Self-assessment

Assessment Type	Purpose	Benefits	Potential Challenges
Open-ended	To gather deep assessment data from students that cannot be obtained using closed-ended questions such as multiple choice, true/false, and fill in the blank questions.	• Teachers get the chance to see the depth and breadth of learning of students. When multiple choice, true/false, and fill in the black questions are asked of students, they provide a small glimpse of what the students know. • Open-ended questions allow for students to provide details and supporting evidence that surrounds their thinking, which can be helpful for teachers as they grade assignments and assess student learning.	• Creating clear, concise, and effective open-ended questions can be difficult. • Unlike multiple-choice questions, it takes a significant amount of time to grade open-ended questions. • There are no specific answers to open-ended questions. Using a general rubric, however, can be helpful.
Peer	The process of partnering with a peer to give them feedback on an assignment that everyone in the class completed.	• Provides students the opportunity to see how other students are thinking about the assignments and responding to them. • Gives students a way to engage with other students and contribute to the class.	• Students may have different levels of content knowledge of the assignment that they are providing their peer feedback on.

Multimedia Platforms **75**

Table 4.1 Cont.

Assessment Type	Purpose	Benefits	Potential Challenges
		• Allows students another chance to connect with the learning content.	• The amount of feedback that each peer will receive from their classmate may vary. • Some students may be too critical instead of constructive in their feedback to their peers.
Self	To think critically about one's own progress and development on an assignment.	• Students can judge their own learning, without feeling the pressures of a peer review or review from the teacher. • Requires students to use their critical thinking skills and reflect on the content at hand. • Students have the chance to use previous assignments to strengthen subsequent assignments.	• Students may have a difficult time accurately evaluating their own progress and may actually undervalue or overvalue the contributions they have made. • Students may not remember what they have accomplished. Conducting self-assessments often and immediately after assignments can help ameliorate this.

76 Multimedia Platforms

Getting at Deeper Learning

In Chapter 1, Bloom's Taxonomy of Educational Objectives (Anderson et al., 2001) was introduced as a framework that provides a hierarchical structure of learning outcomes levels. The "lower level" educational objectives of knowledge, understanding, and application was presented. In this chapter, we move the focus to the "upper level" educational objectives that focus on analysis, evaluation, and creation. Through open-ended assessments, students can demonstrate that they are able to analyze, evaluate, and create content, as well as "draw upon mastery of core content, think critically, and persist in their effort to solve complex problems" (Wren, 2019, p. 14). Because these types of assessments "require varying degrees of student self-directedness, collaboration, and communication" (Wren, 2019, p. 14), they are deeper learning assessments and should be incorporated into our assessment practices. We want to not only determine what students know, but also the depth of that learning.

The first level of the upper level of Bloom's Taxonomy is analysis. Students have already learned new content, came to an understanding, and applied it in some way. At the analysis stage, students would break down the material, organize, and make comparisons and connections. An assessment that is focused on whether students have met the analysis stage could require students to analyze a case study. Case studies could be presented on an editable electronic document so students can use highlighting, drawing, and commenting tools to mark up the case and differentiate the various sections. At the evaluation stage, students must be able to judge content, while prioritizing, justifying, and making decisions. An assessment that is focused on whether students have met the evaluation stage could involve students making judgments and critiquing through a debate or an argumentative essay. Using a digital tool, these can be recorded as audio instead of being text-based. At the highest level of Bloom's Taxonomy, students are charged with creating. When students create, they put together the learning of concepts to craft new ideas and products. Assessments that are focused on whether students have met the creation stage will require

Multimedia Platforms **77**

students to plan, design, and invent. Project and performance-based assessments within makerspaces that require students to reorganize parts and structures, and use elements in news ways, would be an appropriate platform for students to demonstrate that they have met the learning objectives at the creation stage. Makerspaces and their use in assessments are covered later in this chapter.

Open-ended Assessment

Open-ended assessments are those with questions that do not always have a specific correct answer as multiple choice, true/false, and fill in the blank assessment question types have. While you may have a rubric to assess if students have successfully responded to the question posed, each response from students will be different. Open-ended assessment questions must be written intentionally, precisely, and in a way that captures the essence of what the teacher is asking the student to demonstrate. Shilo (2015) provides insights on formulating good open-ended assessment questions by stating "the action verbs must be clear and not ambiguous and direct the examinee to the right answer. Writing statements instead of questions should be avoided, and if statements are used they should be accompanied by detailed instructions" (p. 30). Being cognizant of these aspects when writing open-ended assessment questions is important to administering high quality assessments. Open-ended assessments go beyond responding to long questions or solving word problems. Below, performance and project-based assessments along with digital alternatives to traditional writing assessments, are discussed as open-ended assessment options.

Performance and Project-based Assessments Using Digital Mediums

Performance and project-based assessments can provide teachers with a robust understanding of what students know and how they came to this understanding by reviewing their process from start to completion. Project-based assessments can assess

78 Multimedia Platforms

students on both the content and skills that they will need in their future work to address larger societal needs. For example, students may need to use a combination of mathematical computation and reading comprehension skills, along with critical thinking and collaboration skills to effectively complete project and performance-based assessments. Using content areas skills along with real-world skills requires coordination, organization, and analyzation, which are all higher level thinking skills. According to the Buck Institute for Education (2021): "Project Based Learning is a teaching method in which students gain knowledge and skills by working for an extended period of time to investigate and respond to an authentic, engaging, and complex question, problem, or challenge" (para. 4). Through a traditional close-ended assessment, it would be difficult to assess students' understanding and ability to address these types of robust problems.

A makerspace is an educational tool that includes low and high tech digital components that can be used for performance and project-based assessment. There are many different definitions for makerspaces, but in this book a makerspace is defined as "a place where young people have an opportunity to explore their own interests; learn to use tools and materials both physical and virtual; and develop creative projects" (Fleming, 2015, p. 5). Makerspaces can be set up in schools or in the home (Taddei & Budhai, 2017), using any materials, textiles, recycled projects, and technology components available.

Makerspaces, performance, and project-based assessments are not restricted to science, technology, engineering, and mathematics (STEM) content and concepts. Students can demonstrate their knowledge through inquiry and creation in makerspaces in a wide variety of content areas. Note that many of these assessments will be interdisciplinary in nature, requiring students to use many of these skills collectively. Table 4.2 provides you with a few ideas on how assessments in English-language arts, mathematics, science, and social studies can be created through the engagement of a makerspace. Think about how these assessment activities might be useful in your classrooms.

Multimedia Platforms **79**

Table 4.2 Performance and Project-based Assessments Through Makerspaces

Subject-Area	Performance and project-based assessments through makerspaces can focus on:
English Language Arts	• Researching components to include in digital narratives focused on students' oral communication • Crafting background materials for set of plays focused on English literature • Creating recorded book trailers introducing the main idea and characters of a book
Mathematics	• Sketching geometric figures on different textiles • Designing models and manipulatives that can be used for the class to solve mathematical equations • Drawing out algebraic expressions using various materials
Science	• Displaying engineering cycles and schemes • Building physical sciences models using 3D printers • Creating mock ecosystems, showing the relationships among each level
Social Studies	• Designing appropriate dress and clothing for different historical eras • Creating documentaries of historical events, people, and locations. • Developing geography landforms and city planning and design models

Digital Alternatives to Traditional Writing Assessments

The teaching and assessment of writing is quite an involved process (Parr, 2013). Writing assessments provide teachers with an understanding of students' ability to communicate their ideas, explain concepts, and decipher meaning. According to the Partnership for 21st Century Learning (2021), also known as P21, communication is a critical learning and innovation skill that students must master in school. A Pew Research study (NEA, 2015) showed that communication is the most important skill

80 Multimedia Platforms

that students should have in order to be successful adults. And while some may argue that other skills such as critical thinking and time management are desired future skills, communication is still in the top six skills that employers desire (Boss, 2019). Traditional writing assignments can be monotonous, long, and uninspiring for students. There are other ways for students to demonstrate their communication skills, beyond these types of assessments. Using multimedia platforms such as podcasts, blogs and vlogs, and digital storytelling can be used as assessments to gather an understanding of students' communications skill level. Not only are these assessments innovative and exciting, but they can also provide teachers with information on students' written and oral communication skills.

Podcasting. A podcast is an audio file that can be downloaded (Young et al., 2021). Podcasts can be used to help students with the process of drafting and editing written documents. Before recording an audio file, students need to write out a script or general outline of the podcast content. Once they have their first draft, they need to edit to fit the estimated recorded time of the podcast. Creating a podcast may also include researching topics, gathering facts, and putting content into their own words, which are additional areas and skills that they could be assessed on. Some podcasts are recorded interviews and, in this case, students need to manage facilitating a discussion with the person they are interviewing. The Anchor website provides the availability to create and distribute podcasts.

Blogging and vlogging. Blogs are web-based writings that are based on themes. A video version of a blog, a vlog, "is a form of blogging for which the medium is video" (Gao et al., 2010, p. 15). Instead of a single written assessment, students could be required to keep active blog and vlog entries, where they will post weekly, monthly, or at certain intervals. Blogs and vlogs are often accompanied by imagery that helps bring out thoughts. Blogs and vlogs can also be an effective alternative platform to expository writing assignments. Through the blog and vlogs, students would be able to explain processes, including facts and figures, in a logical and sequential order. The digital tool Weebly has free templates with easy drag and drop features that can house blogs and vlogs.

Digital storytelling. A digital story compiles short vignettes through a multimedia combination (Beck & Neil, 2021). Storytelling is an important writing vehicle for students to learn. Adding digital components with images, music, video, and text can aid in bringing out the main idea and tone of the story in interesting and unique ways. Students can write their stories first and then translate them into a digital story. Using a multimedia application such as Storybird can provide beautiful imagery for digital stories and provide a platform for peer and instructor feedback.

TechAssess Ideas for the Inclusive Classroom

There are different multimedia platforms that can be used for open-ended assessment, which include accessibility features to support English language learners and neurodiverse students with completing open-ended assessments. Table 4.3 provides an overview of the accessibility features of two such multimedia platforms, Seesaw and Nearpod.

Table 4.3 TechAssess Ideas for the Inclusive Classroom

Seesaw is a robust student engagement platform where teachers can upload assessments that students complete. For families whose home language is different from the teacher's or the language the school uses for instruction, notes, captions, comments, announcements, and messages that are posted on Seesaw can be translated into over 55 languages. Since Seesaw is often used for asynchronous learning and independent work time, it will be helpful for families to be able to read over the instructions and support their student at home. Seesaw also has diction and speech-to-text capabilities.

Nearpod is an interactive formative assessment platform. For students who struggle with written directions, there is an audio-recording feature where teachers can provide directions to students using their voice instead of typing. Nearpod also offers a variety of question types and has a drawing tool feature where students can respond to assessment questions by doodling a picture, words, and thoughts.

Peer Assessment

Peer assessment provides students with opportunities to receive feedback on their academic work, from a peer who has completed the same assignment. There are many different definitions of peer assessment but, in general, it is "an assessment method in which students are actively involved in the assessment process" (Rotsaert et al., 2018, p. 76). It is important to note that peer assessments includes "an arrangement for learners to consider and specify the level, value, or quality of a product or performance of other equal-status learners" (Topping, 2018, p. 1). Ketonen et al. (2020) have recognized the potential of peer-assessment practices to advance student learning, as well as the varied benefits peer-assessment can bring students. Depending on several factors, including how much knowledge of the content is being assessed when students are engaged in peer assessment, they have an additional opportunity to look at the content and think through the concepts from a different perspective.

Peer assessments work really well with open-ended assessments, as each student would have approached responding to the questions differently. This would give the student who is assessing their peers' work an example of a different way of responding to the question. There are often multiple ways of solving problems or getting to an answer. Having varied pathways to problem solving when responding to open-ended assessments has tremendous value for students and, through peer assessments, students will have the chance to intently understand this. Using digital tools to facilitate peer assessment can provide students a safe space to give authentic, immediate feedback to each other. Oftentimes, students may be uncomfortable with providing feedback in person; using digital technologies allows students to provide feedback to peers anonymously, thus greatly reducing the pressure on them and avoiding negative impacts (Wang et al., 2017). In addition to providing anonymity to the peer-assessment process, digital tools can provide a safe way to exchange assignments with the tools to leave text, audio, and video comments directly on the paper or submitted assignment.

To prepare students for the peer-feedback process, teachers should model the peer-assessment process. This can be

Multimedia Platforms **83**

accomplished in the way feedback is provided to students, the use of similar rubrics, and through a scaffolded (Vygotsky, 1978) approach. Regardless of grade level, it is best to be sure that students are prepared and able to effectively provide their peers with feedback on an assessment. Scaffolding the peer-assessment process would require the teacher to model and explain how to conduct a peer assessment, followed by engaging in the peer-assessment process as a class, and ending with students getting practice of the peer-assessment process independently. Peer assessments also help prepare students for giving, receiving, and utilizing feedback they will experience in the workforce (Tsai, 2009).

Effective peer assessment is not a "one-off" experience. It should be conducted regularly, embedded in the fabric of the classroom environment and culture. Students will learn by seeing their teachers' model giving feedback to them. Students may need assistance with getting started with the peer-assessment process. Table 4.4 provides ideas and digital tools for peer-assessment starters across grade bands.

Table 4.4 Ideas and Digital Tools for Peer-assessment Starters Across Grade Bands

Grade Band Level	Description
Elementary	Using editable documents through a digital tool such as Google Docs is a simple and effective way to provide students with a format to give peer feedback. For younger students, the Google Doc could have a statement such as "My peer partner's sentence was....." and then the options could be simple words such as "great", "good", "fair" or with emoji faces that correspond to those words. A combination of words and emojis could be used as well, which would be helpful to students as they would see both the words and images that represent them. Since the Google Doc can be easily edited from any location or device in real time, questions can be added and modified depending on the peer-assessment assignment, without taking too much time for you as the teacher to prepare.

(*continued*)

84 Multimedia Platforms

Table 4.4 Cont.

Grade Band Level	Description
Middle	For middle school students, providing an editable questionnaire type form through a digital tool such as Google Forms could be useful. As the teacher, you could create a series of closed and open-ended questions for the peer to respond to, based on their partner's work. The close-ended questions could be on a Likert scale
	that ranges from agree to disagree. There can also be open-ended questions that will allow for more narrative feedback. Starter sentences can be provided for the open-ended questions focused on, so that middle school peers can give substantive narrative feedback. For example, a start sentence could be "You did a good with ....". The peer would have to pull out the evidence of the items their peer was successful at demonstrating.
High	High school students could use a digital tool such as Padlet, which would provide them with the space to exchange assessments and provide feedback. A padlet allows for the uploading of documents, images, and audio. Text can also be typed directly on a padlet where students can provide peer feedback. Since high school students would have more experience with writing, they may be able to benefit from a "sandwich" approach, where more constructive feedback is nestled between positive and affirming comments.

Tips for Setting up Peer Assessment

There are many ways to organize peer-assessment teams. Instead of pairs, you may want trio peer-assessment teams. In this case, student A provides feedback to student B, who provides feedback to student C. Student C would provide feedback to student A. Each student would get feedback from a peer, but they will not provide feedback to the person who gave them feedback. Doing peer assessment in this way may remove some of the pressures that exist with a one-to-one exchange. If the peer-assessment process is not anonymous, there are likely virtual

Multimedia Platforms   **85**

conferencing tools within your school's learning management system (LMS) that can be used. If your LMS does not have a virtual conferencing tool, you can utilize a free tool such as Zoom. Regardless of whether you set up the peer assessment in pairs, trios, or another format, it is imperative that students know what they are looking for in terms of providing feedback. Providing students with starter sentences like the ones provided in Table 4.4, along with the assignment rubric and checklists, would be helpful. Table 4.5 provides two from the From the Field TechAssess examples that use the digital tools Flipgrid and Padlet for peer assessment with authentic tasks.

Table 4.5 From the Field TechAssess Example

Overview: To track learning and to check for understanding and assess specific skills of my students.

Skills Being Assessed: Pronunciation, fluency, sentence structure, vocabulary

Digital Tools Used: Flipgrid

Why I Use the Digital Tool to Assess Student Learning: Students would have prepared a script in French that is inclusive of the major themes of the unit (rubric and directions would be provided). They would then share (present) that script to their peers and teacher in class and respond to peer/teacher questions. Language learners often lack confidence when speaking the "new" language. They may feel awkward and are worried about sounding "funny" and/or making mistakes. In the digital format, students are provided with time to plan and practice when speaking the target language (in this case, French). It also helps eliminate some of the nervous jitters around speaking in front of their peers. Even though their classmates will view the videos, they have the time to seek out help and make changes before presenting their video. In this way, they can be more confident that they did a good job before sharing their videos with the class and teacher.

Other Ideas: Peer feedback can be provided to the students by their classmates and their teacher through Flipgrid as well. Students and the teacher can comment on the presentations with text or video.

Teacher: Barbara Hanes, 9–12th Grade French, Malvern, Pennsylvania

----

Overview: In order to assess students' "jots" (things they notice/wonder/connect) when reading, I created a Padlet, linked to my virtual classroom.

(continued)

86 Multimedia Platforms

Table 4.5 Cont.

Skill Being Assessed: Students' ability to comprehend, make connections to, and record their thinking while reading realistic fiction books independently.

Digital Tools Used: Padlet

Why I Use Digital Tools to Assess Student Learning: Kids would have been writing their ideas on post-it notes and sticking them to the pages of their books as they read. I would then ask them to take their last five jots and stick them to a piece of paper so I could review/assess them. Covid made me need to find a way to review their thinking from a distance. But additionally, I wanted kids to be able to read peer examples to help them develop more complex interpretations of the text by learning from one another and building upon each other's ideas.

Other Thoughts: The free version of Padlet has a lot of great functions. If I want to truly assess learning, I can make it so posts need to be approved before other students can see them. This prevents kids from just copying another student's response.

Teacher: Adam Dalicandro, 4th Grade, Andover, Massachusetts

Self-assessment

Self-assessment provides an opportunity for students to reflect on their learning and "encourages the learner to take an active role in the educational process, making him or her reason their own strengths and weaknesses which, in turn, empowers the student as an active learner" (Gurbanvo, 2016, p. 83). There are many definitions and understandings of self-assessment (Brown & Harris, 2013) and in agreement with Andrade (2019), "This very broad conception might seem unwieldy, but it works because each object of assessment—competence, process, and product—is subject to the influence of feedback from oneself " (p. 2). This suggests that there are many conceptualizations of self-assessment; this text uses one of these.

For the purposes of this section of the book, self-assessment is two-fold. First, self-assessment is the process of students checking their own understanding of content, concepts, and processes. This occurs through a broad range of self-assessment activities.

Multimedia Platforms **87**

Second, self-assessment is the process of students reflecting on their own learning, identifying areas of needed growth, and using that information to impact future assessments. Aligned with the focus of this book on leveraging digital tools to assess student learning, what follows is reflective of this conceptualization. It is important to note that both types of self-assessment connect to students' cognitive presence, and critical thinking skills and dispositions (Garrison et al., 2001).

QR Codes to Checking One's Own Understanding

Short for "quick response", QR codes can be described as "two dimensional images composed of small black squares. A free QR codes scanner app can read the spaces between the black dots and take you to information stored on the web" (Burns, 2016, p. 8). QR codes can be used in K-12 settings for self-assessment and the checking of one's own understanding. Students can use a variety of different technology devices with a camera to scan the QR code, which can take them to text, a website, a video, audio, and other resources. Students can complete assessment activities and use QR codes to check on how they did. QR codes are easy to set up and can be used year after year in your classroom. In Table 4.6, eight examples of self-assessment through QR code activities in English-language arts, mathematics, science, and social studies are shared. As you read through the examples, make a note of the self-assessment activities using QR codes that you would like to incorporate in your own classroom.

Table 4.6 Self-assessment QR Code Activities

English-language arts	• **Vocabulary**: Students can check their vocabulary knowledge by reading through various definitions of vocabulary words and scanning a QR code to check if their responses are correct. On the reverse of that, for older students in particular, students could have a list of vocabulary words which they would say to themselves the definition and then scan a QR code to check if they recited the correct definition.

(*continued*)

88 Multimedia Platforms

Table 4.6 Cont.

	• **Parts of speech**: Students could check their understanding of different parts of speech, by scanning QR codes that, when scanned, will reveal if the words on their list were correctly categorized as a noun, verb, adverb, adjective, etc.
Mathematics	• **Algebraic equations**: Students could complete a variety of math problems with complexity varying depending on grade level. Students could work through the problems and then scan the QR codes to see the answers. The QR codes could also lead to visuals showing the proper steps for completing the problems. • **Word problems**: Students could complete word problems and scan the QR codes and review the correct answers against their answers. Word problems can be quite complex, and the QR codes could also lead to audio-recorded explanations of how the correct answer was solved.
Science	• **Ecosystems**: Students can be given terms that are connected to the ecosystem and asked to provide an accurate description. Once they have recorded their answer, they can scan the QR code to check to see if they are correct. Or, instead of a description, students could be shown a picture of the interconnectedness of different parts of the ecosystem and asked to name what the picture is showing. They would then scan the QR code to see the correct answer and check against theirs. • **Solar system**: Students can be given a description of different planets within the solar system and then scan a QR code that would lead to text or an image that corresponds with the description of the solar system to check that they are correct.
Social studies	• **History**: Students can be given an important date in history and asked what event happened that day, or why that day is significant. They would then scan the QR code to check if their response is correct. • **Geography**: Students can be asked to be given a capital of a state and be asked to name what state the capital is in, or the reverse of that, where students are given the state and asked to name the capital. They would check the QR to determine if they are correct.

Multimedia Platforms **89**

Voice-recordings and Video for Self-assessment and Reflection

In addition to engaging in self-assessment activities where students check their own understanding of learning, self-assessment also involves reflecting on one's own learning in order to decipher outcomes of their own work and plan for subsequent efforts. Harris and Brown (2018) identified four areas that self-assessment address including:

1. guiding students to a deep understanding of appropriate standards for judging the quality of work;
2. helping them understand how to evaluate their performance against those standards;
3. assisting them to arrive at a realistic understanding of their performance or work; and 4. teaching them to interpret and use these data in ways that.

(p. 2)

All of these areas can be developed by not only thinking out loud through the recording of self-reflections on performance of an assessment, but also by using video to view oneself in practice. Voice-recording and use of video to self-reflect on learning creates a dynamic and powerful mechanism for thinking about how one has met learning goals. Since most knowledge is tacit, in order to come to and understanding of how much content has been learned, students must actively reflect on their learning to activate knowledge (Schön, 1983). A digital tool such as VoiceThread can "be especially helpful at increasing student engagement and motivation while activating learning" (Brunvand & Byrd, 2011, p. 28). On VoiceThread, the students can use video and audio for a more immersive and authentic reflective self-assessment. A summary of perceived learning through a more animated reflection can be done through a digital tool such as PowToon.

Video-recorded presentations can provide students with additional feedback and helpful information about their work during the self-assessment process (Ritchie, 2016). The assessment of presentations can range from using a speaking and listening rubric such as Palmer's (2021) PVLEGS (poise, voice, life, eye

90 Multimedia Platforms

contact, gestures, and speed), or the actual depth and articulation of the content being presented. Effectively presenting materials to the teacher and class can be a daunting experience. Allowing students to video record themselves while presenting affords them the chance to see what others see, determine if they have met the learning objectives, and practice their presentation skills. In order for students to effectively go through the stages of cognition, they need to be open and honest with their experiences (Taddei & Budhai, 2015, p. 43), which can be done through video and voice-recorded self-reflection. Students can use the digital tool VoiceThread to record their presentations.

Experiential Activities for Open-ended, Peer and Self-assessment

Learning happens through practice and experience (Dewey, 1938; Kolb, 1984; Vygotsky, 1978). When students have the chance to connect with content and concepts through experiential learning activities, they develop their content knowledge and critical-thinking skills across subject areas. Digital tools can serve as a catalyst for students to engage in a host of experiential learning activities and, through this, teachers can formatively assess their learning of different subjects through students' engagement in virtual labs, simulations, and virtual field trips and tours.

Why have students complete worksheets when they can explore new lands through virtual and augmented reality tools? It is difficult to travel nationally and internationally to some of the interesting places that students learn about in their social studies, history, and geography courses. Instead of having them fill in a blank map or answer questions about different places, why not have them virtually tour these new environments, while identifying the specific components that they have learned about in your classes? Students can engage in virtual simulations and teachers can see how they navigate through the experience, notate areas that students may need further support on, and provide students with the necessary feedback to develop in specific areas.

Virtual labs and online simulations can be assigned to students as ways to demonstrate their ability to follow multi-step directions of a process and can serve as a way for students to engage in an experiential learning assessment activity. Virtual labs can be described as "an e-learning tool wherein software simulates the experiment and the learner follows a path of discovery-based learning rather than that of verification-based learning" (Sharma & Ahluwalia, 2018, p. 2). Virtual labs and online simulations in this respect are an open-ended, experiential assessment that can also be a self-assessment activity as well. Students can record themselves working through a lab assignment, where they are dissecting an animal or insect or safely compounding chemicals with adult supervision. In online simulations, students receive experiential learning experience that incorporates deeper learner and prepares them for solving real-world problems (Zhu et al., 2018). The PhET website offers free game-like math and science simulations. Peer assessment could also be incorporated. Peer teams can go through simulations together, as one student identifies specific components as directed by their teacher, a peer can take notes on the other student's progress; or, at the end of the simulation, provide feedback to the peer on their performance.

Virtual field trips and tours provide a great way to expose students to places, people, and artifacts around the world. Instead of teaching students about the ancient methodology through textbooks, students can virtually visit museums or see 3D and 360-degree images, to help bring the content to life. There are many cost-effective options for virtual field trips and tours through the Smithsonian Museum, Google Arts and Culture content, and the Google Treks Maps site. Teachers can test students' knowledge and understanding of concepts by providing them with a checklist of things to cover during their virtual field trip and tour. Peer-assessment activities can require peers to check that their partner's checklist is completed. Teachers can also provide students with open-ended guided questions to gauge their thinking around the different topics, what they are seeing, and how they are making sense of it. Students can self-reflect on their experiences as well.

92 Multimedia Platforms

Now What? How to Get Started

Now that you have been introduced multimedia platforms for open-ended, peer and self-assessment, the next step to get started is to decide on which one you would like to start with. You can certainly offer all three assessment types, but I recommend you start with one first. Table 4.7 provides a few tips on the steps to take to get started with gathering data through open-ended assessments, providing peer-assessment opportunities in your class, and giving students the chance to engage in self-reflection.

Table 4.7 Tips for Getting Started with Open-ended, Peer, and Self-assessment

Open-ended assessment

Step 1: Determine the content and skills that you are assessing the student on.

Step 2: Choose type: performance-based, project-based, or experiential.

Step 3: Explore digital tools that students could potentially use.

Step 4: Create a rubric to appropriately assess learning (*we discuss rubrics in Chapter 5).

Peer assessment

Step 1: Determine which assignment would work best for peer assessment.

Step 2: Create peer assessment pairs or teams.

Step 3: Provide a virtual space for assignment exchange and review.

Step 4: Give guidance on how peers can use peer feedback for future assignments.

Self-assessment

Step 1: Determine if students will check their own understanding or reflect on their learning.

Step 2: Develop the peer-assessment activity or reflection guidelines.

Step 3: Choose the appropriate digital tool for the activity or reflection in step 2.

Step 4: Review the data from the self-assessment activity.

Related Resources and Digital Tools

In Table 4.8, additional resources and digital tools that can be used for open-ended, peer, and self-assessment are listed. Many of these tools are mentioned with some suggestions for their use throughout this chapter. An overview of each tool and URL address are provided to assist you as you peruse them.

Table 4.8 Related Resources and Digital Tools

Name	Overview	URL
Open-ended Assessment Tools		
Anchor	Online platform for podcast creation and distribution	https://anchor.fm
Buck Institute for Project-based Learning	Website with resources on designing, implementing, and assessing project-based learning	www.pblworks.org/what-is-pbl
Google Arts and Culture	Virtual interactive experiences related to cultures around the world	https://artsandculture.google.com
Google Maps Treks	Integrated street view maps with cultural, historical, and geographic significance	www.google.com/maps/about/treks/#/grid
Makerspace	Website that houses information on makerspaces in education	www.makerspaces.com/what-is-a-makerspace
Nearpod	Multimedia platform for interactive formative assessment within lessons	https://nearpod.com/
PhET	Free math and science simulations from the University of Colorado Boulder	https://phet.colorado.edu/

(continued)

94 Multimedia Platforms

Table 4.8 Cont.

Name	Overview	URL
Seesaw	Student engagement platform that houses assessments	https://web.seesaw.me/
Smithsonian National Museum of Natural History	Virtual tours connected to K-12 curriculum and learning goals	https://naturalhistory.si.edu/education/school-programs
Storybird	Creative writing digital platform focused on developing writing skills for young learners	https://storybird.com
Peer Assessment Tools		
Flipgrid	Video discussion tool	https://info.flipgrid.com/
Google Docs	Collaborative smart editing of documents tool	www.google.com/docs/about/
Google Forms	Web-based survey tool	www.google.com/forms/about/
Padlet	Digital boards that can house multimedia content with tools for providing text, audio, and video feedback	https://padlet.com/
Zoom	Video-conferencing tool with share screen and chat features	https://zoom.us
Self-assessment Tools		
QR Code Generator	Free platform to create QR codes	www.qr-code-generator.com
VoiceThread	Multimedia tool that can be used for voice-recorded reflections and student presentations	https://voicethread.com
PowToon	Visual and video communication platform	www.powtoon.com

Summary

Effective assessment of student learning involves more than the use of traditional tests such as multiple choice, fill in the blank and true/false questions. Assessments need to go beyond the lower level of Bloom's Taxonomy and assess students' ability to analyze, create, and evaluate. By leveraging the various digital tools within multimedia platforms, teachers can create robust and exciting open-ended assessments, focused on performance and project-based tasks, and provide alternatives to traditional assignments. Through peer assessments, students have the chance to get feedback from each other, have the opportunity to revisit previously learned content, and can see other ways of problem-solving. Finally, self-assessments are critical aspects of the assessment cycle and allow students to engage in critical reflection about their own learning, and use the information they learned about themselves to impact future assignments. I hope that you will be inspired by the From the Field TechAssess examples and try one using a multimedia platform for open-ended, peer, and self-assessment. In the next chapter, the focus is on using digital tools to curate, evaluate, and disseminate evaluation data.

References

Anderson, L.W., Krathwohl, D.R., & Bloom, B.S. (2001). *A taxonomy for learning, teaching, and assessing: A revision of Bloom's Taxonomy of educational objectives* (Complete ed.). Longman.

Andrade, H.L. (2019). A critical review of research on student self-assessment. *Educational Psychology and Methodology*, 4(87), 1–13.

Beck, M.S., & Neil, J. (2021). Digital storytelling: A qualitative study exploring the benefits, challenges, and solutions. *CIN: Computers, Informatics, Nursing*, 39, 123–128.

Boss, S. (2019). It's 2019. So why do 21st-century skills still matter. *EdSurge.* www.edsurge.com/news/2019-01-22-its-2019-so-why-do-21st-century-skills-still-matter.

Brown, G.T., & Harris, L.R. (2013). Student self-assessment. In: McMillian, J. (ed.) *SAGE handbook of research on classroom assessment.* Thousand Oaks, CA: Sage (pp. 367–393).

96 Multimedia Platforms

Brunvand, S., & Byrd, S. (2011). Using voicethread to promote learning engagement and success for all students. *TEACHING Exceptional Children*, 43(4), 28–37. https://doi.org/10.1177/004005991104300403.

Buck Institute for Education (2021). What is PBL? www.pblworks.org/what-is-pbl.

Burns, M. (2016). *Deeper learning with QR codes and augmented reality: A scannable solution for your classroom*. Corwin.

Dewey, J. (1938). *Experience and Education*. The Macmillan Company.

Fleming, L. (2015). *Worlds of making: Best practices for establishing a makerspace for your school*. Corwin.

Gao, W., Tian, Y, Huang, T., & Yang, Q. (2010). Vlogging: A survey of videoblogging technology on the web. *ACM Computing Surveys*, 42(4), 1–57.

Gardner, H. (1983). *Frames of mind*. Basic Books.

Garrison, D.R., Anderson, T., & Archer, W. (2001). Critical thinking, cognitive presence and computer conferencing in distance education. *American Journal of Distance Education*, 15(1), 7–23.

Gurbanvo, E. (2016). The challenge of grading in self and peer-assessment (undergraduate students' and university teachers' perspectives). *Journal of Education in Black Sea Region*, 1(2), 83–91.

Harris, L.R., & Brown, G.T.L. (2018). *Using self-assessment to improve student learning*. Routledge.

Ketonen, L., Hähkiöniemi, M., Nieminen, P., & Viiri, J. (2020). pathways through peer assessment: Implementing peer assessment in a lower secondary physics classroom. *International Journal of Science & Mathematics Education*, 18(8), 1465–1484.

Kolb, D.A. (1984). *Experiential learning: Experience as the source of learning and development*. Prentice-Hall.

National Education Association. (2015). The most important skill for students? Communication, most Americans say. www.nea.org/advocating-for-change/new-from-nea/most-important-skill-students-communication-say-most-americans.

Overton, T. (2012). *Assessing learners with special needs: An applied approach*. Pearson.

Palmer, E. (2021). The PVLEGS story. https://pvlegs.com/the-pvlegs-story-2/.

Parr, J.M. (2013). Classroom assessment in writing. In: McMillian, J. (ed.) *SAGE handbook of research on classroom assessment*. Thousand Oaks, CA: Sage (pp. 489–501).

Partnership for 21st Century Learning. (2021). P21 network. www.battelleforkids.org/networks/p21.

Ritchie, S.M. (2016). Self-assessment of video-recorded presentations: Does it improve skills? *Active Learning in Higher Education*, 17(3), 207–221. https://doi.org/10.1177/1469787416654807.

Rotsaert, T., Panadero, E., & Schellens, T. (2018). Anonymity as an instructional scaffold in peer assessment: its effects on peer feedback quality and evolution in students' perceptions about peer assessment skills. *European Journal of Psychology of Education*, 33(1), 75–99. https://doi.org/10.1007/s10212-017-0339-8.

Sharma, S., & Ahluwalia, P.K. (2018). Can virtual labs become a new normal? A case study of Millikan's oil drop experiment. *European Journal of Physics*, 39(6), 1–18.

Schön, D. (1983). Design as a reflective conversation with the situation. In *The reflective practitioner: How professionals think in action* (pp. 76–104). Basic Books.

Shilo, G. (2015). Formulating good open-ended questions in assessment. *Educational Research Quarterly*, 38(4), 3–30.

Sienkiewicz, E. (2018). What does a performance assessment look like? Here are 6 examples. Center for Collaborative Education. www.cce.org/thought-leadership/blog/post/performance-assessment-six-examples.

Taddei, L., & Budhai, S.S. (2015). Using voice-recorded reflection to increase cognitive presence in hybrid courses. *Journal of Digital Learning in Teacher Education*, 32(1), 38–46.

Taddei, L., & Budhai, S.S. (2017). *Nurturing young innovators: Cultivating creativity in the classroom, home, and community*. Portland, OR: International Society of Technology in Education (ISTE).

Topping, K. (2018). *Using peer assessment to inspire reflection and learning*. Routledge.

Tsai, C. (2009). Internet-based peer assessment in high school settings. In: Tan Wee Han, L., & Subramaniam, R. (eds) *Handbook of research on new media literacy at the K-12 level: Issues and challenges*. Hershey, PN: IGI Global (pp. 743–754). https://doi.org/10.4018/978-1-60566-120-9.ch046.

Vygotsky, L. (1978). *Mind in society: Development of higher psychological processes*. Harvard University Press.

Wang, X.-M., Hwang, G.-J., Liang, Z.-Y., & Wang, H.-Y. (2017). Enhancing students' computer programming performances, critical thinking awareness and attitudes towards programming: An online peer-assessment attempt. *Educational Technology & Society*, 20(4), 58–68.

Wren, D.G. (2019). *Assessing deeper learning: Developing, implementing, and scoring performance tasks*. Rowman & Littlefield Publishers.

98 Multimedia Platforms

Young, B., Pouw, A., Redfern., A., Cai, F., & Chow, J. (2021). Eyes for ears – a medical education podcast feasibility study. *Journal of Surgical Education*, 78(1), 342–345.

Zhu, M., Panorkou, N., Lal, P., Etikyala, S., Germia, E., Iranah, P., Samanthula, B., & Basu, D. (2018). Integrating interactive computer simulations into K-12 earth and environmental science. *2018 IEEE Integrated STEM Education Conference (ISEC)*, 220–223. https://doi.org/10.1109/ISECon.2018.8340488.

5

Online Tools to Curate, Evaluate, and Disseminate Assessment Data

Using Assessment Data to Guide Instructional Practices

We have reached the final chapter of this book. Once assessment data are collected by leveraging a wide variety of digital tools, the information should be used to guide instructional practices. According to the National Center for Education Evaluation and Regional Assistance (2009), data of student achievement can help teachers in the following ways:

- prioritizing instructional time
- targeting additional individual instruction for students who are struggling with particular topics
- more easily identifying individual students' strengths and instructional interventions that can help students continue to progress

DOI: 10.4324/9780429345517-5

100 Online Tools

- gauging the instructional effectiveness of classroom lessons
- refining instructional methods
- examining schoolwide data to consider whether and how to adapt the curriculum based on information about students' strengths and weaknesses (p. 5).

Because of the rich, robust, and dynamic nature of digital tools, teachers will have access to not only student scores, but trends and patterns of student learning and gaps that need to be addressed. With this type of information, teachers will be able to use assessment data to differentiate instruction for students, identify students who may need additional support, and use the information to reflect on their own practice.

Differentiating Instruction

One of the most useful aspects of using digital tools to assess student learning is the ability to access individualized data on student achievement. Student data informs differentiated instruction through a planned process (Faber et al., 2018), and having data on students is critical for planning for instruction that meets the needs of all students. Whether students are answering questions through online polling or virtual quizzing, or using multimedia online platforms to demonstrate their knowledge, teachers will have individual data on each student in the class. Knowing how students learn and the areas in which they thrive or need more support in, can help teachers differentiate instruction to meet the individual needs of students.

When teachers differentiate instruction, they address variances that learners have through content, process, product, and learning environments changes (Tomlinson, 1995). Not only does differentiating instruction for students have the potential to impact their academic success (Smale-Jacobse, 2019), it will also provide a mechanism to ensure that learning happens in a positive and conducive way. One of the positive impacts of leveraging digital tools to assess student learning is being able to use them to differentiate instruction. Table 5.1 provides ideas

Online Tools 101

on how to use digital tools to differentiate content, process, and products (Tomlinson, 1995), to meet the individual learning needs of all students in your classroom.

Table 5.1 Using Digital Tools to Differentiate Instruction

Content	Process	Products
Provide a variety of ways for students to access the curriculum materials including audio, visual, and text-to-speech options. Use breakout rooms and pair students to virtually work in teams.	Develop learning activities that go beyond listening to lectures. Offer students choice in experiencing virtual labs, simulations, and project-based learning. Give students the chance to inquire, discover, and create through makerspaces.	Design assessments using modifiable virtual tools such as Google Docs and Google Forms. For multiple-choice questions, modify the question types depending on student needs. Offer digital word banks or fill in the blank questions.

Reflecting on Practice

We discussed the importance of reflection and student self-assessment in Chapter 4. It is equally important for teachers to reflect on their own practice and self-assess their own teaching. Reflection goes beyond just thinking about instruction, and involves problem-solving, inquiry, and the development of solutions (Murray, 2015). Because of this, reflecting on teaching is quite critical. In fact:

> The complexity of teaching requires teachers to question their practices for their own professional development in order to improve and to increase learner performance. Reflective practice is the ability to reflect on an action so as to engage in a process of continuous learning. A key rationale for reflective practice is that experience alone does not necessarily lead to learning; deliberate reflection on experience is essential.
>
> (Mathew et al., 2017, p. 126)

102 Online Tools

The teaching day often goes by quite expeditiously, with not much time to stop to reflect. One digital tool that may help teachers capture in real time their notes on how instruction is going, improvement areas to focus on, and general observations is a voice memo feature on a smartphone (Kamal, 2020). Most teachers have a smartphone, tablet, or even a computer with audio memo capabilities. Analyzing student data in concert with listening to reflections can be impactful for reflective practitioners, in a process that Schön (1983) describes as reflection-in-action.

Curation Tools to Organize Assessment Data

Digital curation has been linked to libraries (Gregory & Guss, 2011), but it also has relevance in K-12 education. In fact, one of the International Society of Technology Education (ISTE) Standards for Educators is to "model for colleagues the identification, exploration, evaluation, curation and adoption of new digital resources and tools for learning" (ISTE, 2021, para. 2). Part of this is being able to curate student assessment data in a way that promotes effective organization, evaluation, and dissemination. One of the challenges to collecting a multitude of data from students, is a way to efficiently organize that data. We want to be able to use the data to make instructional decisions; however, it is difficult to do so if the data is not within reach and accessible. Not only should the data be available to teachers to review, it should be organized in a way that teachers can easily access specific types of data that they are looking for (Barnes & Fives, 2020).

The National Research Council (2015) has noted that digital curation among professionals in different fields is varied. However, there are many benefits to curating content digitally. Digital tools such as multimedia curation platforms, intuitive digital spreadsheets, and video storage sites can assist with the organization of assessment data. Free curation tools are also widely available on the internet (Sharma & Deschaine, 2015).

YouTube has been used as a social technology for professional development (Copper & Semich, 2014), and can also serve as a curator of student presentations and other video-recorded assessment data. Table 5.2 provides more details on video storage curation options such as Viemo. Some of the benefits of digital curation of content include:

Space: Digital curation of assessment data eliminates the need of having to physically store a large amount of data in boxes and file cabinets. Physically storing assessment data year after year can become taxing and eventually there will not be enough room remaining to house student work. With online storage, as files grow, more storage can be easily obtained in the cloud.

Access: When assessment data is curated using digital tools, it becomes extremely accessible. Teachers will be able to access student data from home, on vacation, or anywhere they have access to a technology device and the internet. Also, teachers can save time sifting through files and papers. The digital nature of curation in this way will allow for searching for specific student names and assessments. Class and student folders can be created and arranged by the school year, assessment type, or other formats that would work best for the teacher's personal organizational style and needs. Having a base with links to the different curated data is key. Multimedia platforms such as Wakelet or Milanote have the capabilities to store, organize, and share content. Table 5.2 provides a description and features of both platforms.

Evaluation: The evaluation process of sifting through hundreds of different types of student assessment data becomes more manageable when using digital tools. There are features within digital spreadsheets like ZohoSheet or Google Sheets that can organize the data by student, getting means, modes, and medians of each assessment. Table 5.2 provides a brief overview of their key features. Also open-ended assessment data that include audio and video features can be housed using multimedia curation platforms.

104 Online Tools

Table 5.2 Curation Tools to Store and Organize Assessment Data

Multimedia Platforms	Intuitive Digital Spreadsheets	Video Storage
Wakelet	**ZohoSheet**	**YouTube**
Description: Online platform that can save, organize, and share content in one place.	**Description:** Online spreadsheet software.	**Description**: Video-sharing platform.
Key features: Ability to bookmark online content from other sites, can house documents, videos, Twitter postings, and blogs.	**Key features:** Automatically cleans up data including removing duplicates, fixes data inconsistencies, and fills in missing values. Collaborative features for teams and works well with Excel files.	**Key features:** Ability to create a channel to house all videos. Videos can be organized by groups with playlists. Also has commenting and sharing capabilities.
Milanote	**Google Sheets**	**Vimeo**
Description: Visual project-board that can house notes, images, and files.	**Description**: Web-based spreadsheet program.	**Description**: Video-hosting platform.
Key features: Ability to change organization of content, leave notes and to-do lists directly on items, and others can be invited to edit.	**Key features:** Has built in formulas, templates, and pivot tables. Explore panel option provides overview of data, summaries, and information from pre-populated charts.	**Key features:** Ability to house videos and create live streams. Has templates to use. Integrates into Google Drive and Dropbox.

There are many other multimedia platforms, intuitive digital spreadsheets, and video storage tools that can be used to curate assessment data. It is also important to note that many multimedia platforms that are used for open-ended assessment can house assessment data within the platform itself. In Chapter 4, the digital tool Nearpod was introduced as an opened-ended assessment tool that has a variety of accessible features for learners who need extra support. Nearpod is also a multimedia platform that teachers can use to house assessment data of their students that was completed through Nearpod. In Table 5.3, a From the Field TechAssess example is provided, showing the inclusion of Nearpod to collect assessment data as well as the additional technologies tools that can be used within Nearpod to house the data. A teacher's Nearpod account, holding the student assessment data collected from the platform, can still be linked to a base curation site through a digital tool such as Wakelet or Milanote, as explained in Table 5.2, so that all of the data can be accessed from one online location.

Table 5.3 From the Field TechAssess Example

Overview: To assess student learning, I use online tools that include a variety of video, visuals, and presentation materials.

Skill Being Assessed: Student comprehension of text

Digital Tool Used: Nearpod

Why I Use Digital Tools to Assess Student Learning: Nearpod makes every lesson interactive. It allows you to create your own lesson by uploading them from Google Slides and other places. Teachers can then present live lessons (synchronously) and student-paced lessons (asynchronously). Nearpod can engage and assess students in real time. All students can be active participants in the learning process. Students would have written responses down on paper or used turn and talk in person.

Other Thoughts: You can present slides, videos, audio, slideshows, do virtual field trips, interactive Sway presentations, Nearpod 3D, do a Live Twitter Stream, and add Web Content

Teacher: Nicole Draper, 4th Grade, Wilmington, Delaware

Anchoring Digital Tools to Evaluate Data

Scanning for issues of academic integrity, using a rubric to gauge the levels of performance in which students have met the assignment criteria, and providing feedback to students are all

106 Online Tools

part of the process of evaluating assessment data. Depending on the assignment, you may pay closer attention to whether the content was from the student and, if it was not, if it was properly cited. Cultivating a culture that is situated within academic integrity may decrease the likelihood of students cheating.

Cultivating Academic Integrity

As the growth of K-12 online learning is increasing exponentially (Barbour & Harrison, 2016), the need for using digital tools to evaluate assessment data will also increase. As we evaluate assessment data and make plans for future instruction and assessments, it is important to consider students' understanding of academic integrity. At a young age, students need to be taught how to properly give credit for the work that they obtained from others.

Preparation: The first way to get ahead of potential issues with academic integrity is to properly prepare students for the assessment. When students feel prepared, they are confident and more likely to do well on the assessment. Use formative assessment measures throughout instruction to check and see where students are with understanding content, before the unit assessments are given. Offer practice questions using the online polling and virtual quizzing tools described in Chapter 2 so students not only get the chance to revisit the content but get practice with answering questions.

Digital citizenship: If you go back to Chapter 3, part of students' development of digital citizenship skills includes understanding what copyright is, and how to give credit for work if they decide to cite someone else's work in their assignments. In addition, students should be critical consumers of content and be able to discern the quality of sources of information found online. Students will often go to Google to search and click on Wikipedia for information. This type of pattern is the opposite of what students should do to obtain quality sources. Providing students access to sites such as Kids Britannica, National Geographics Kids, Smithsonian Learning Lab, and other educational research databases for older students, can provide quality sources for obtaining online content to cite.

Continuity in citing sources: Citing sources should be a constant in the classroom. Teachers should cite sources and have a reference page for all online lectures and materials provided to students. Modeling for students how to cite sources, and providing them consistent opportunities to see citations in action, will be helpful as students develop their own facility with citing sources.

Plagiarism software: When students reach middle and high school, you may want to use plagiarism software such as Turnitin and Plagiarism Checker X to check their writing assignments for uncredited content. Students may not even realize that they are not citing sources properly and having the software can show students the percentage of their writing that was copied. This may be helpful in reducing future plagiarism. Students can also use the plagiarism checker by Grammarly to upload papers into the system and check if there are too many consistencies with other published works on over 16 billion web pages.

Utilizing Online Rubrics

As the evaluation of assessment data takes place, utilizing an online rubric can be helpful with the efficiency of grading, and provide students and their families with specific information about their performance on assessments. A rubric is "a scoring tool that lays out the specific expectations for an assignment. Rubrics divide an assignment into its component parts and provide a detailed description of what constitutes acceptable or unacceptable levels of performance for each of those parts" (Stevens et al., 2005, p. 3). A rubric can accompany many types of assessments and are often used for writing, presentation, and project and performance-based assessments. Rubrics can also be used for peer and self-assessments. While you would not necessarily need to use a rubric for assessments with a set of algebra questions, for a science question asking how many planets there are, or even a spelling test, offering a rubric could certainly help guide students' work and provide a fair way to score and grade the assessment.

Table 5.4 illustrates a sample layout of a rubric. With the use of digital tools such as Rubric Maker and Quick Rubric, rubrics with the same format as seen in Table 5.4, can easily be created

108 Online Tools

online. Online rubric applications have libraries of editable templates, pull-down criteria features, and the ability to export the rubrics as PDF and Excel files. Having rubric templates saved online provides quick access for editing rubrics for students who may have different performance criteria. For self- and peer assessments, a digital tool such as ForAllRubrics offers student accounts with checklists and badges. The format of the rubric in Table 5.4 can be used for different types of assessments and the contents would depend on the actual assessment goals. The criteria column would be filled in with the aspects of the assessment in which students should demonstrate competency. Rating levels can be changed as you see fit, with descriptions of the different levels of performance for each of the respective criteria.

Table 5.4 Sample Layout of a Rubric

CRITERIA	RATING LEVEL			
	EXCELLENT	VERY GOOD	GOOD	POOR
		DESCRIPTIONS OF PERFORMANCE ON ASSESSMENT FOR EACH CRITERIA, AT EACH RATING LEVEL.		

You can craft the different criteria of different assessments based on the learning goals. Table 5.5 provides ideas of what the criteria could be for a few of the open-ended assessments that were discussed in Chapter 4. These are provided to give you an idea of the possible areas of performance to focus on, but is by no means an exhaustive list. You may choose to have more or less than three criteria for each as well. You would also need to break down each criterion by the performance levels that you choose (excellent, very good, good, poor).

Online Tools **109**

Table 5.5 Rubric Criteria Examples for Open-ended Assessments

Opened-ended Assessment Type	Criteria		
Makerspaces	A variety of materials used	Corresponding inquiry report completed	Final product aligns with learning goal
Podcasts	Length of podcast recording was within specified guidelines	All required content covered	Quality of written draft script prepared before recording
Simulations	Simulation completed in its entirety	Completeness of corresponding note sheet	Comprehensiveness of self-reflection on experience
Virtual field trips	Full attendance of virtual field trip	Completeness of virtual field trip report	Peer feedback on virtual field trip report provided

Digital Provision of Feedback

Providing feedback to students on their performance is critical to their continued growth and development. Knowing which questions were answered correctly provides preliminary data for students, but knowing more details and, more importantly, how to approach answering questions in subsequent assessments is key. Providing and receiving feedback can be a difficult task, but as long as it is constructive and value-added, students can benefit from it. We should also focus on students' strengths (Galloway et al., 2020), and the assets that they bring to the assessment. Then, value-added feedback can be provided that helps students build on their strengths and to work on the areas in which they need further development.

Digital tools can be helpful with providing feedback to students that goes beyond "good job" or a letter or numeric grade with no narrative comments. Through the use of digital tools, feedback can be provided through track changes, audio, video, and live feedback. Table 5.6 provides more information on how to do each and shares a potential technology that can be used in doing so.

110   Online Tools

Table 5.6 Using Digital Tools to Provide Feedback

Feedback Type	Digital Tool	Description
Tracked comments	Taut	Instead of providing feedback using typed narrative comments on assignments at the end of the paper, presentation, or project, using a digital tool such as Taut will allow comments to be dragged and dropped over the different parts of the assessment that the comments are referring to. You can also include links to additional resources that students can leverage to improve future assessments.
Audio	Kaizena	Sometimes it is helpful to hear the tone of the voice of the person who is providing feedback, as opposed to reading typed feedback and trying to imagine how the person was intending to share the comments. Using a digital tool such as Kaizena, will allow for feedback to be recorded as audio clips and attached to the assessment. If you find yourself giving the same type of feedback to students on formatting, structure, and general writing guidelines, you can save those and attach them on each student's paper, where applicable.
Video	Explain Everything	Providing video feedback comments provides students the benefits of the integrative and audio comments. Using a website such as Explain Everything can allow teachers to use screencasting technology to make a video and provide feedback to students. This may be particularly helpful with explaining assessments that involve processes.
Live/Virtual	Video conferencing tool available within your school's LMS	It may be helpful to meet with students and provide them feedback in a virtual, live setting. For example, you could share your screen with students and show them their performance on a virtual quiz through Kahoot! by showing them their report, as in Figure 5.1.

Online Tools 111

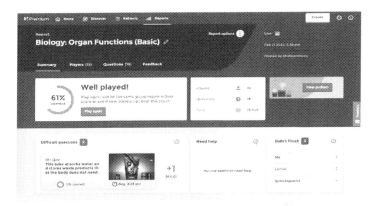

Figure 5.1 Kahoot!
Source: Kahoot!
Note: Kahoot! and the K! logo are trademarks of Kahoot! AS

Now What? How to Get Started

Now that we have covered using digital tools to assess, curate, evaluate, and disseminate student data, the next step is to get started with choosing which digital tools you will use to capture different types of data, to house the data, to evaluate the data, and to share the data. There are individual tools that do one or some of these different aspects of the assessment process. Figure 5.2 is an image illustrating the different elements of the Yacapaca assessment tool. If you choose a tool such as this, you would be able to: encourage students' self-assessment checks, collect formative data from students, encourage students to complete different assessments, send parents reports of their students' progress, and practice concepts that they need support on. The Yacapaca assessment tool is unique because it uses gamification to encourage students to go and complete more assessments, check answers, and provide feedback to peers all in one tool.

112 Online Tools

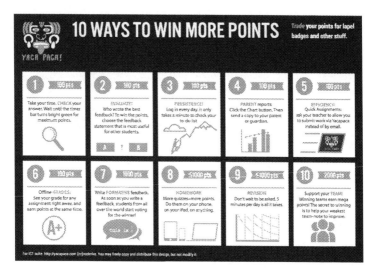

Figure 5.2 Yacapa Assessment Application Elements
Source: Ian Grove Stephensen, (cc no derivs) yacapaca.com.

Virtual Dissemination of Assessment Data

To make the best use of assessment data beyond modifying instructional practices, you should disseminate it to the families of students as well as the administration. It is important to know the audience that assessment data are being disseminated to (Brownson et al., 2018) since this would impact the purpose of sending assessment data, what assessment data you send and the format you send it in. Data are very multifaceted and can be complicated to understand if the purpose is not clearly communicated.

Sharing Student Learning with Families

The Harvard Family Research Project (2013) acknowledges that while there are traditional ways of sharing data with families such as through parent–teacher conferences and quarterly report cards, more frequent means of data sharing is necessary to provide families with continued monitoring of their children's progress. Additionally, while grades on report cards provide a cumulative sense of where students are in general terms, they do not provide specificity on the areas of learning that students are well developed in, or that need more attention. If families are only updated on their child's learning a few times per year, they will not be able to properly support their learning needs on a consistent basis. One of the benefits of using digital tools to assess student learning is the ability to seamlessly share data with families. Many of the digital assessment tools discussed throughout this book offer reports of student progress to families. The reports would be automatically emailed to parents after completion of the assessments, to keep families informed of student progress throughout the school year. An alternative to sending out reports individually from the different online assessment tools is to upload student progress into one site such as Fresh Grade. The Fresh Grade online application allows families to track student progress of different types of assessments and communicate with teachers regarding their child's progress.

Student websites can serve as digital portfolios that will house a summative collection of student work throughout the year. Google Sites offers free websites with templates that can easily be used across K-12 grade levels. Having student websites where key artifacts and signature assignments can be posted and shared with families is a way to communicate progress to parents. With student websites, multimedia assessments that incorporate audio, video, and images can be shared. Through a digital tool such as Kidsblog, only the teacher and families would see the work, and weekly assessments can be posted to keep families informed. Students and their families, in concert with the teacher, can look at all work within the digital portfolio and make a plan for further growth and development. By disseminating student data to families on a consistent basis, they will always have access to see how their children are making progress and meeting their learning goals.

114 Online Tools

Collecting Cumulative Class Data for Administration

The administration has many uses for student data. Administrators may use assessment data to make decisions on curriculum programs and plan for professional development for teachers (Dyer, 2016). Having the assessment data of the students in your class may help your administration as they prepare annual and periodic reports to external state and federal accrediting agencies. The school district your school is housed within may also ask for data from each class to make comparisons with other schools in the district. Also, grants and other funding sources are often tied to assessment data. Having student data on hand will be helpful to administrators if funding opportunities emerge where they can quickly pivot and use the data to make a case for why particular interventions and instructional changes are required.

By using a digital tool such as Microsoft Excel Online, summative class data can be put together quickly for administrators. Microsoft Excel Online has many options to share individual and class data through charts and graphs and display the tracking of student scores over time. You may also want to use the class data from an open-assessment digital tool such as Nearpod to show the time it took students to answer questions, the questions skipped most, and the most difficult questions for the class.

As you evaluate and disseminate the students' data, and find out which types of assessment work best for students, you may begin to make modifications. To ensure that each student is offered the chance to demonstrate their knowledge using a form of assessment that meets their individual learning styles, a framework such as Universal Design for Learning (CAST, 2018) could be employed. More specifically, provide students with multiple means of action and expression to show what they know through the utilization of digital tools. Table 5.7 describes the areas of the Universal Design for Learning, Multiple Means of Action and Expression category.

Table 5.7 UDL's Multiple Means of Action and Expression with the Use of Digital Tools

TechAssess Ideas for the Inclusive Classroom

Utilizing Universal Design for Learning can provide students with multiple means of action and expression, and support how students plan and perform tasks, as guided by the following three areas:

Physical action: Providing different options for students to physically answer questions. Use touchscreen tablets and laptops as well as well as different mouse click options. Alternative keyboards, and voice-to-text applications should be available. Be flexible with the time provided to students between responding to assessment questions.

Expression & communication: A wide variety of multimedia tools should be used for students to share their learning including, but not limited to, images, audio, text, drawings, storyboards, social media technologies, and manipulatives. Supportive aides such as spell checkers, sentence starters, and concept-mapping tools should be available.

Executive functions: Prepare students for success with assessments by modeling, scaffolding, and providing exemplars. Include prompts for students that encourage them to stop and think through thoughts before responding to assessment questions. Offer checklists, note-taking templates, graphic organizers and rubrics to guide performance. Offer continued opportunities for self-monitoring and self-reflection.

Related Resources and Digital Tools

There were several digital tools mentioned throughout the chapter. Table 5.8 provides a list of those digital tools with corresponding URLs, organized by category. Feel free to use them as you curate, organize, evaluate, and disseminate your students' assessment data.

116 Online Tools

Table 5.8 Related Resources and Digital Tools

Name	URL
Data Curation & Organization Tools	
Google Sheets	www.google.com/sheets/about/
Milanote	https://milanote.com
Vimeo	https://vimeo.com/
Wakelet	https://wakelet.com
YouTube	www.youtube.com
ZohoSheet	www.zoho.com/sheet/
Academic Integrity Tools	
Britannica Kids	https://kids.britannica.com/
Grammarly	www.grammarly.com/
National Geographic Kids	https://kids.nationalgeographic.com/
Plagiarism Checker X	https://plagiarismcheckerx.com/
Smithsonian Learning Lab	https://learninglab.si.edu/
Turnitin	www.turnitin.com/
Online Rubric Makers	
ForAllRubrics	www.forallrubrics.com
Quick Rubric	www.quickrubric.com/
Rubric Maker	rubric-maker.com/
Assessment Feedback Tools	
Explain Everything	https://explaineverything.com
Kaizena	www.kaizena.com
Taut	www.tautapp.co
Dissemination Tools	
Fresh Grade	https://freshgrade.com/
Google Sites	https://sites.google.com/
Kidsblog	https://kidblog.org/
Microsoft Excel Online	www.office.com

Summary

In order to make full use of student assessment data, it must be properly curated, evaluated, and disseminated. Teachers can make instructional decisions, differentiate content, process, and products associated with instruction, and self-reflect on their practice if they have access to organized and meaningful assessment data. By leveraging digital tools, assessment data can be efficiently organized within multimedia platforms, intuitive digital spreadsheets, and online video storage solutions. Data can be evaluated through online rubrics to assess student performance. Feedback can be provided to students using tracked comments, audio recordings, video messages, and live virtual meetings. Finally, digital tools can be used to share student data with families and administrators. I hope that you have found the content of this book useful as you leverage digital tools to assess student learning.

References

Barnes, N., & Fives, H. (2020). *Managing classroom assessment to enhance student learning.* Routledge.

Brownson, R.C., Eyler, A.A., Harris, J.K., Moore, J.B, Tabak, R.G. (2018). Getting the word out: New approaches for disseminating public health science. *Journal of Public Health Management and Practice*, 24(2), 102–111. doi: 10.1097/PHH.0000000000000673.

CAST (2018). *Universal design for learning guidelines version 2.2.* Wakefield, MA: Author.

Copper, J., & Semich, G. (2014). YouTube as a teacher training tool: Information and communication technology as a delivery instrument for professional development. *International Journal of Information and Communication Technology Education*, 10(4), 30–40. https://doi.org/10.4018/ijicte.2014100103.

Dyer, J. (2016, January 19). Three ways to put assessment data to work in the classroom. NWEA. www.nwea.org/blog/2016/three-ways-to-put-assessment-data-to-work-in-the-classroom/.

Faber, J.M, Glas, C.A.W., & Visscher, A.J. (2018). Differentiated instruction in a data-based decision-making context. *School Effectiveness and School Improvement*, 29(1), 43–63.

Galloway, R., Reynolds, B., & Williamson, J. (2020). Strengths-based teaching and learning approaches for children: Perceptions and practices. *Journal of Pedagogical Research*, 4(1), 31–45. https://doi.org/10.33902/JPR.2020058178.

Gregory, L., & Guss, S. (2011). Digital curation education in practice: Catching up with two former fellows. *The International Journal of Digital Curation*, 2(6), 176–194.

Harvard Family Research Project (2013). *Tips for administrators, teachers, and families. How to share data effectively*. https://archive.globalfrp.org/var/hfrp/storage/fckeditor/File/7-DataSharingTipSheets-HarvardFamilyResearchProject.pdf.

International Society of Technology Education (2021). ISTE Standards for Educators. www.iste.org/standards/for-educators.

Kamal, J. (2020). *Making time for reflective practice*. Edutopia. www.edutopia.org/article/making-time-reflective-practice.

Mathew, P., Mathew, P., & Peechattu, P.J. (2017). Reflective practices: Means to teacher development. *Asia Pacific Journal of Contemporary Education and Communication Technology*, 3(1), 126–131.

Murray, E. (2015). Improving teaching through collaborative reflective teaching cycles. *Investigations in Mathematics Learning*, 7(3), 23–29.

National Center for Education Evaluation and Regional Assistance (2009). Student Achievement Data to Support Instructional Decision Making. https://ies.ed.gov/ncee/wwc/Docs/PracticeGuide/dddm_pg_092909.pdf

National Research Council (2015). *Preparing the workforce for digital curation*. Washington, DC: The National Academies Press. https://doi.org/10.17226/18590.

Schon, D. (1983). Design as a reflective conversation with the situation. In Schon, D. (ed.) *The reflective practitioner: How professionals think in action*. Basic Books (pp. 76–104).

Sharma, S.A., & Deschaine, M.E. (2015). The five Cs digital curation: Supporting twenty first century teaching and learning. *InSight: A Journal of Scholarly Teaching*, 10, 19–24.

Smale-Jacobse, A.E., Meijer, A., Helms-Lorenz, M., & Maulana, R. (2019). Differentiated instruction in secondary education: A systematic review of research evidence. *Frontiers in Psychology*, 10, 2366. https://doi.org/10.3389/fpsyg.2019.02366.

Stevens, D., Levi, A., & Walvoord, B. (2005). *Introduction to rubrics: An Assessment tool to save grading time, convey effective feedback, and promote student learning*. Stylus Publishing.

Tomlinson, C. (1995). *How to differentiate instruction in mixed-ability classrooms*. Association for Supervision and Curriculum Development.

Index

Note: Page numbers in *italics* indicate figures and in **bold** indicate tables on the corresponding pages.

academic growth 3–4
academic integrity 105–107, **116**
all of the above questions 40
Anchor 80, **93**
Answer Garden **44**
app **50**
Articulate360 **10**, **19**
artificial intelligence **50**
assessment: in the 21st century 1–3; defined 2; of diverse learners 11, 13, **14**; dual purposes of 2; influence of technology on practices in 5–11, *7*, *8*, **10**; multimedia platforms in (*see* multimedia platforms); promoting the 4Cs and entrepreneurial thinking 6–9, *7*, *8*; for quickly discovering gaps 15; real-time instructional modifications using 3, 15–16, 114; standards alignment 3–4; student engagement embedded in 9–11; of students without them knowing they are being assessed 6; through questioning (*see* questioning); through social media, memes, and emojis (*see* social technologies); as tracking of academic growth 3; types of 11, **11–13**; *see also* data, assessment
AudioBoom **10**, **19**
automatic saving **14**
avatar **50**

Backchannel Chat **69**
benchmark assessment 11, **12**
bitmoji **50**, **68**
blogging 8, **10**, 11, 20, 80

120 Index

Bloom's Taxonomy of Educational Objectives 36–37, 37, **39**, 73, 76, 95
Boom Cards 33–34, **33**, **44**
Britannica Kids 106, **116**
Brown, G. T. L. 87, 89
Buck Institute for Education 78
Buck Institute for Project-based Learning **93**

Cameras on Chromebooks **55**
Chandler-Olcott, K. 61
chatbots 50, **65**, **66**, **69**
Children's Online Privacy Protection Rule (COPPA) 20, 67
Child's Internet Protection Act (CIPA) 20, 67
citing of sources 106–107
cognitive presence 5, 87
collaboration 2, 8–9, **10**
communication: appropriate 52–53; skills in 2, 7–8, **8**, **10**
Community of Inquiry Model 5
content consumption 53
copyright 53, 106
Creative Commons 50
creativity 2, 9, **10**
critical thinking 2, 6–7, **7**, **10**, 73, 75, 78, 80, 87
Crowd Signal **44**
curation, digital 102–105, **103**, **105**, **116**

data, assessment: academic integrity and 106–107, **116**; administration collection of cumulative class 113–114; anchoring digital tools to evaluate 105–108, **108**; curation tools to organize 102–105, **103**, **105**, **116**; differentiated instruction and 100–101, **101**; digital provision of feedback and 108–109, **110**, *111*, **116**; getting started with digital tools for 111, *112*; online rubrics and 107–108, **108**, **109**, **116**; reflecting on practice and 101–102; related resources and digital tools 114, **116**; sharing student learning with families and 112–113, **116**; used to guide instructional practices 99–102; virtual dissemination of 111–112; *see also* assessment
Department of Education, US 4
diagnostic assessment **11–12**
differentiated instruction 100–101, **101**
digital citizenship 20, 50, 52–53, 106
digital KWL charts 15
digital storytelling 9, **10**, 11, 80–81
digital tools: academic integrity and 106–107; anchored to evaluate data 105–108, **108**; facilitating Universal Design for Learning 16–17; game-like tools using 6; influence on assessment practices 5–11, **7**, **8**, **10**; integrated directly into lessons 15; legal and ethical considerations with 17–19; promoting the 4Cs 6–9, **7**, **8**, **10**; related resources and 19, **19–22**; role in leveling the playing field for assessing diverse learners 11, 13, **14**; in student-guided tracking of learning 16; tips for getting started with using **18**; transforming assessment practices with 13–17
direct message (DM) **50**, 56
Discrepancy Model 16
dissemination tools 112–113, **116**
diverse learners, assessment of 11, 13, **14**
double-barreled questions 40

Index   **121**

Edublogs 20
elementary school level: emojis as assessment tools at 63–65, 66; memes to demonstrate learning at 61–63; peer assessment at 83; questioning tools at 41
Emojicopy 68
emojis 63; as assessment tools in early elementary classrooms 63–65, 64; defined 50, 64; *see also* social technologies
emoticons 51, 65, 66, 68
entrepreneurial thinking 6–9, 7, 8
Epic! 7, 7, 20
Every Student Succeeds Act (ESSA) 4–5
Explain Everything 110, 116

feedback, digital provision of 108–109, 110, *111*, 116
Field TechAssess 7, 7, 8, 34, 55, 85–86, 105
field trips, virtual 91–92
fill in the blank questions 38
filters 51
Fine, S. 25
Flipgrid 85, 94
ForAllRubrics 108, 116
formative assessment 12–13; questioning in 26
4Cs 2, 6–9, 7, 8, 10
Fresh Grade 113, 116

Gardner, H. 49
Garrison, D. R. 5
geotags 51
Glossary of Education Reform 2
Google Arts and Culture 91, 93
Google Docs 11, 20, 94
Google Forms 94
Google Maps and Treks 91, 93
Google Sheets 104, 103, 116
Google Sites 113, 116
Google Translate 20
Grammarly 107, 116

handle 51
Harris, L. R. 87, 89
Harvard Family Research Project 112
hashtags 51
high school level: memes to demonstrate learning at 63; peer assessment at 84; questioning tools at 41
Hinchman, K. 61

iCivics 8, 20
iEmoji 68
Iloveimg 69
Imgflip 62, 69
infographics 9, 21
International Literacy Association 61
International Society of Technology Education (ISTE) 102
Isaacs, D. 61

Jeopardy Labs 6, 21
Journal of Adolescent & Adult Literacy 61

Kahoot! 6, 21, 32, 44, 110, *111*
Kaizena 110, 116
Kapwing 69
Ketonen, L. 82
Kialo 9, 10, 21
Kidsblog 113, 116
Knovio 10, 21
Kulasegaram, K. 4
KWL charts 15

labs, virtual 91
legal and ethical considerations with digital tools 17–19
Listenwise 9, 10, 21
Lumen5 69

Makerspace 77, 78, 79, 93, 109
makerspaces 77–78, 79, 93, 101, 109

122 Index

Mathew, P. 101
Mehan, H. 26
Mehta, J. 25
memes: defined **51**; to demonstrate learning 61–63; as digital assessment tool 61–63; meme generators **51**, 62, **69**; *see also* social technologies
Mentimeter 45
Meyer, A. 2
Miao **66**, **69**
microblogging **51**, **69**
Microsoft Excel Online 114, **116**
middle school level: memes to demonstrate learning at 63; peer assessment at **84**; questioning tools at 41
Milanote **104**, 103, **116**
mind-mapping 7
Mindmeister **10**, **21**
multimedia platforms: curation tools 102–105, **104**; deeper learning and 73–76, **74–75**; as digital alternatives to traditional writing assessments 78–81; experiential activities and 90–92; introduction to 72–73; open-ended assessment and **74**, 76–81, **79**, **81**; peer assessment and **74–75**, 81–85, **83–86**; performance and project-based assessments using 77–78, **79**; related resources and digital tools 93, **93–95**; self-assessment and **75**, 86–90, **87–88**; tips for getting started with **92**, 92
multiple choice questions 38

narrative explanations **14**
National Association for the Education of Young Children (NAEYC) 64
National Association of Secondary School Principals 48
National Center for Educational Evaluation and Regional Assistance 99
National Geographic Kids 106, **116**
National Research Council 102
Nearpod 17, **21**, **81**, **93**, 104, **105**
negative phased questions 40
none of the above questions 40
notifications **51**

Online Exit Tickets **21**
online polling: advantages of 29–30; anonymity of responses in 30–31; considerations when creating 30–32, **35**; defined 27; limited devices in 31; onboarding for 31; purpose of 27; time limits for 31–32; types of 27; used across different grade bands 40–42, **42–43**; uses of 28–29, 29
online simulations 91
open-ended assessment **74**, 77; digital alternatives to traditional writing assessments and 78–81; experiential activities for 90–92; performance and project-based, using digital mediums 77–78, **79**; related resources and digital tools 93, **93–94**; tips for getting started with **92**, 92
open-ended questions 39

Padlet **84–86**, **94**
Palmer, E. 90
parental consent for social technology use 67
Partnership for 21st Century Learning **22**, 78
peer assessment **74–75**, 81–83; across grade bands **83–84**; experiential activities for

Index 123

90–92; related resources and
digital tools 92, **95**; tips for
getting started with **92**, 92;
tips for setting up 84–85,
85–86
performance and project-based
assessment 77–78, **79**
performance tasks 7
PhET 91, **93**
Piktochart **10, 21, 22**
Pinterest 58, **59, 69**
Plagiarism Checker X 107, **116**
plagiarism software 107
podcasting 8, 11, **19**, 80, 80
Poll Everywhere 41, **45**
polling *see* online polling
Poore, M. 54
PowToon **89, 95**
PraxiLabs **22**
privacy 52, 66
Prodigy Game 7, **7, 22**
project-based assessments 77–78,
79
ProjectPals **22**
Proprofs **44**
PVLEGS 89–90

QR codes 87, **87–88, 95**
questioning: across different
grade bands 40–42, **42–43**;
Bloom's Taxonomy of
Educational Objectives and
36–37, 37; creating quality
questions for 34, 36–37,
37, **38–39**, 40; in formative
assessment 26; online polling
27–32, 29, **35**; reasons for
using 25–26; related resources
and digital tools for 43, **44–46**;
types of 26, **26**, 37, **38–39**;
virtual quizzing 32–34, **34–36**;
what to avoid in quiz 37, 40
Quick Rubric 107, **116**
Quizizz 41, **45**
Quizlet **45**

quizzing, virtual *see* virtual
quizzing

Rangachari, P. K. 4
real-time instructional
modifications 15–16
reflecting on practice 101–102
respectful behaviors 53
Response to Intervention (RTI)
Model 16
Ribble, M. 52
Rose, D. 2
Rubric Maker 107, **116**
rubrics, online 107–108, **108,
109, 116**

safe practices in digital
citizenship 52
Schön, D. 102
Seesaw **81, 94**
self-assessment **75**, 86–87;
experiential activities for
90–92; QR codes in 87, **87–88**;
related resources and digital
tools 93, **96**; tips for getting
started with **92**, 92; voice-
recordings and video for 87,
89–90
Shilo, G. 76
Sienkiewicz, E. 73
Slido 29, **45**
Smart Learning Suite 7, **7, 22**
Smiley.cool 68
Smithsonian Learning Lab 106,
116
Smithsonian Museum 91, **94**
social media: checking students'
understanding through 55–60,
57, 59; defined **51**; as digital
assessment tool 53–55, **55**;
Pinterest 58, **59**; setting up
safeguards for 65; sites for
68–69; TikTok 60, **60**; Twitter
51, 56–58, **57**; *see also* social
technologies

124 Index

social technologies: definitions related to 50, **50–51**; digital citizenship and **20**, **50**, 52–53; related resources and digital tools 68–69, 69; role in assessment practices 48–49; setting up safeguards with 65; *see also* memes; social media
Socrative **46**
spreadsheets, digital 102–105, **104**
Storybird **10**, **22**, **81**, **94**
student engagement 9–11
student-guided tracking of learning 16
summative assessment **13**

Taut **110**, **116**
teaching, reflecting on 101–102
TechAssess **68**, **81**, **115**
technology *see* digital tools
test anxiety 6
text highlighting **14**
text to speech **14**
3D printed models 9
TikTok 55, 60, **60**, **68**, **69**
Tinkercad **10**, **22**
translation tools **14**
true/false questions **39**
Turnitin 107, **116**
Tweets **51**
Twitter **51**, **54**, 55–56, **57**, **68**, **69**, 104–105

Universal Design for Learning (UDL) 2, 11, 16–17, **22**, 114, **115**

Vevox **46**
video for self-assessment 87, 89–90
video storage curation tools 102–105, **104**
Vimeo **104**, **116**
virtual field trips 91–92
virtual labs 91
virtual quizzing: advantages of 33–34, **33–34**; defined 32; purpose of 32; types of 32–33, **35–36**; used across different grade bands 40–42, **42–43**
visuals **14**
vlogging **51**, 80
voice-recordings: for presentations 8; for self-assessment 87, 89–90
VoiceThread 89, **95**

Wakelet **104**, 103, **116**
Weebly 80–81
writing assessments, digital 78–81

Yacapaca **46**, 111
YouTube 102, **104**, **116**

ZohoSheet **104**, 103, **116**
Zoom 85, **94**